A SHIELD
AND HIDING PLACE

A SHIELD AND HIDING PLACE

The Religious Life of the Civil War Armies

BY

GARDINER H. SHATTUCK, JR.

MERCER UNIVERSITY PRESS

ISBN 0-86554-273-2 (cloth)
ISBN 0-86554-346-1 (paper)

A Shield and Hiding Place:
The Religious Life of the Civil War Armies
Copyright © 1987
Mercer University Press, Macon GA 31207
All rights reserved
Printed in the United States of America
Second Printing December 1988

The paper used in this publication meets
the minimum requirements of American National Standard
for Information Sciences—Permanence of Paper
for Printed Library Materials, ANSI Z39.48-1984.

Library of Congress Cataloging-in-Publication Data
Shattuck, Gardiner H.
A shield and hiding place.
Originally presented as the author's thesis (Ph.D.)—
Harvard University, 1985.
Bibliography: p. 137.
Includes index.
1. United States—History—Civil War, 1861-1865—
Religious aspects. 2. United States. Army—Religious
life—History—19th century. 3. Confederate States of
America. Army—Religious life. I. Title.
E635.S48   1987   973.7'78   87-11157
ISBN 0-86554-273-2 (cloth)   (alk. paper)
ISBN 0-86554-346-1 (paper)

CONTENTS

To

Cynthia

In God is our trust,
he will help us in all times of need.
Oh Lord if we should go into battle,
be thou our shield & hiding place.
If it is consistent with thy will,
that any of us should be killed,
may we have a happy admittance
into thy Kingdom above.

WILLIAM RUSSELL,
26TH VIRGINIA REGIMENT

(Diary entry, 2 April 1864, in the William Russell Papers, Manuscript Department, Duke University Library, Durham NC.)

PREFACE

This book originated as a doctoral thesis written in the early 1980s at Harvard University. As with any piece of historical scholarship, my work has inevitably been influenced by social and cultural forces shaping the country as a whole during the period when it was composed. Rather than asking the reader to guess my prejudices and presuppositions, I believe that it is more beneficial to confess them at the outset. Although such candor may leave me open to the charge of presentism and perhaps undercut the supposed objectivity of my judgments, I think that honesty about my biases is warranted here.

When I began the research that resulted in this book, I decided that I would study the response of the churches to the Civil War, and through that examination draw some conclusions about the relationship of religion and culture in America. At first, I expected to find chauvinism and religious thought so hopelessly entangled during the Civil War that they could never be separated. I felt sure that I was going to fault the American churches, and especially the churches in the South, for abandoning their moral autonomy in order to bless the war effort of the region they supported. I no longer wish to make that judgment, since the impact of religion on the war was, in fact, subtle and variegated—sometimes hampering and sometimes bolstering militaristic pretensions. My respect for religion in the South, moreover, has markedly increased since I worked on this study. I have learned that the message preached by the Southern churches, while by no means denying the culture altogether, provided some individuals with psychological distance from it and from the cultural assumptions that many Southerners held.

This reappraisal of the South by a Northerner like myself, however, should not be entirely surprising, for the popular image of the South has changed considerably in the past few years. The poor, violent, racist South of the 1960s has been transformed twenty years later into a prosperous, friendly, religious, and even racially tolerant society. It is now respectable in the academic world to be sympathetic towards the antebellum South—kindly disposed at least to the intellectual bases of its thought. Of course, no one defends the virulent racism of some Southern slaveholders, but Southern mores no longer seem utterly counter to the rest of the American way of life either before or after 1860. The decline of the popularity of political liberalism, as well as the nostalgic wish for the return to simple, old-fashioned, rural virtues, has made the South appear more attractive in intellectual and popular circles than at any other time in the last fifty years.

We in the post-Vietnam era also see in the postbellum South heretofore unrecognized features of American life. Besides the optimistic image now projected by the states of the so-called Sun Belt, the South has been noted, too, for the tragic, pessimistic world view that it at one time fostered. The South knew frustration, failure, and guilt in the wake of its defeat in the Civil War, and Southerners for a time felt out of step with the Northern myths about the inevitability of victory and progress for Americans. Yet today the Confederacy no longer is unique in its inability to win a war. The story of the South's recovery of its self-esteem after military failure projects a remarkably familiar quality to all Americans.

Although I started this project in academia, I did not finish it there, and my vocation as a parish minister has similarly affected my outlook on my subject. As someone who regularly attempts to interpret Christian theology and history in a pastoral context, I have been distressed by two recent trends in American religion that have had deleterious effects on church life. These trends have been nurtured and given their shape by the television evangelists. Neither of these ways of thinking is new to the present day, but each has received an extraordinary impetus via the American media. The first I call the gospel of success, the idea that the acceptance of the Christian faith always enables men and women to lead prosperous and successful lives. The history of the churches in the nineteenth-century South is, I think, an antidote to that notion. The second trend that I deplore is the effort by evangelical Protestants to grasp political power and control in order to mold American society in their own images of rectitude. In this regard, too, the leadership of the Moral Majority has lost touch with its Southern religious roots.

I would like to add one further autobiographical note. Like so many who are fascinated by the Civil War, nothing pleases me more than visiting the Civil War battlefields maintained by the National Park Service. The Park Service is to be wholeheartedly commended for its efforts not only in preserving these historic sites, but also in making the history of the Civil War accessible to so many Americans. The single aspect of the war that the Park Service has failed to highlight, however, is the impact of religion on the soldiers. Orientation films and shows at visitor centers never note how important religion was in providing inspiration, consolation, and even distraction from the ennui of camp life. Civil War soldiers gathered in great numbers around campfires to participate in revivals, not just to see minstrel shows. If this book is ever bought by a visitor to Gettysburg, Antietam, or elsewhere, I hope that it will enable that person to have a better (if only slightly so) understanding of the Civil War.

I am indebted to many people for their help with this project. I am grateful to the following libraries for their permission to quote from manuscripts in their collections: the Manuscript Department of the Duke University Library, the Southern Historical Collection of the University of North Carolina at Chapel Hill, the Department of Archives of the Jessie Ball DuPont Library of the University of the South, the Houghton Library of Harvard University, and the Andover-Harvard Theological Library of Harvard Divinity School. I also owe thanks to the following institutions for permission to reproduce photographs, portraits, and illustrations in their possession: the Library of Congress, the University of the South, the Civil War Library and Museum in Philadelphia, and the Press of Morningside Bookshop.

I would like to thank my thesis advisors, William R. Hutchison and David Herbert Donald, for their assistance on the original composition of this manuscript at Harvard. They provided me with meticulous editing and incisive criticism, and whatever errors I have made in this work are due only to my inability to follow their fine scholarly advice.

I would like the following friends and colleagues to know how much I appreciate the encouragement they gave me while I worked on this book: Mark Massa, my fellow doctoral student at Harvard, who offered me numerous thoughts and ideas about this topic during our many meals together; Marie Cantlon, who acted as my agent, brought this manuscript to Mercer University Press, and secured a publishing contract for me; and the staff of the Andover-Harvard Library, parishioners of Epiphany Parish, Walpole, Massachusetts, and parishioners of the Church of the Ascension, Cranston, Rhode Island, all of whom watched me put this book together during the time that I worked with them, and always showed interest in and support for my project.

Finally, greatest thanks of all go to family members who have been constantly exposed to my work: my father and mother, who have shown great delight and pride at seeing their son's thoughts in print; my daughter Rachel, who at eight years old wonders why her father so enjoys a topic that she finds both uninteresting and terrible; and my wife Cynthia, who

has amiably tolerated my preoccupation with nineteenth-century America, who has given innumerable comments on my work, who has contributed many weeks of her time and her own professional skill in carefully
editing this book, and who has provided me with inestimable emotional
support—in gratitude for which I have dedicated this book to her.

Gardiner H. Shattuck, Jr.
Cranston, Rhode Island
September, 1986

INTRODUCTION
Religion and Regional Cultures in Nineteenth-Century America

Writing to his father in January 1861, Charles C. Jones, Jr., of Georgia expressed his despair about the irreconcilable differences dividing the two sections of the United States. On the eve of the Civil War, Jones, like many other Southerners, feared that those differences were sufficient justification for dissolving the Union and forming a new nation. He even went so far as to say that there were actually two American races, "which, although claiming a common parentage, have been so separated by climate, by morals, by religion, and by estimates so totally opposite to all that constitutes honor, truth, and manliness, that they cannot longer exist under the same government." The consensus of beliefs, attitudes, and expectations that once had bound the American people together had been dissipated by the impact of divergent secular and religious trends in the first half of the nineteenth century. By 1861 religion, formerly a common element that united Northerners and Southerners, had become one of several ideological factors responsible for exacerbating the sectional conflict.[1]

Although the religious heritage of the majority of Southerners and Northerners was represented by the broad consensus of evangelical Protestantism, this tradition had broken apart in American in the 1830s, and its regional components had been diverging since then. Formal divisions within the Presbyterian, Baptist, and Methodist denominations acted as a prelude to the later political divisions of the country and helped make the military

---

[1]Robert Manson Myers, ed., *The Children of Pride: A True Story of Georgia and the Civil War* (New Haven: Yale University Press, 1972) 648; Carl N. Degler, *Place Over Time: The Continuity of Southern Distinctiveness* (Baton Rouge: Louisiana State University Press, 1977) 60; and John W. Kuykendall, *Southern Enterprize: The Work of National Evangelical Societies in the Antebellum South* (Westport CT: Greenwood Press, 1982) 160.

conflict irrepressible. Slavery, of course, forced the breach between the churches. Many Northern evangelicals viewed the South as a region of barbarity and irreverence, a land blighted by the odium of slavery, where true religion could never be practiced. For their part, Southern Christians replied with a strong critique of the deplorable religious state of the North. They claimed that instead of fostering Christianity, the Northern churches harbored a dangerous religious heterodoxy that sought its basis not in the Bible, but in shameful and irresponsible movements for social reform. Christians of both sections denounced the churches of the other region as being riddled with corruption and praised their own religious bodies for maintaining a humble and godly spirit, the essence of the gospel.[2]

The most important theoretical disagreement between religion in the North and religion in the South concerned the responsibility of the churches for the morals of their society. Northern and Southern evangelicals upheld fundamentally differing views about the relationship of faith and society. Northern evangelicals envisioned holiness as touching the whole nation, and they reflected that vision in numerous organizations for moral reform created to perfect both the individual and the nation. Their goal was a truly Christian nation, composed of moral individuals, that would carry out the will of God not only in America, but also throughout the world. Southern evangelicals had no vision comparable to that of their counterparts in the North. Southern Christians' essential religious mission placed emphasis only on the morality of individuals; it had little relevance for the moral condition of their society. They eschewed changing the world, but settled instead for transforming the individual. To have done otherwise, they thought, would have challenged the sovereignty of God.[3]

---

[2]Samuel S. Hill, Jr., *The South and the North in American Religion* (Athens: University of Georgia Press, 1980) 73-74, 78-79, 87-88; Bertram Wyatt-Brown, *Southern Honor: Ethics and Behavior in the Old South* (New York: Oxford University Press, 1982) 103-105, 341-42, 348; Kuykendall, *Southern Enterprize*, 20-21, 150-51, 162-63, 165, 168-69; Sandra Sizer, "Politics and Apolitical Religion: The Great Urban Revivals of the Late Nineteenth Century," *Church History* 48 (1979): 88-89; Donald G. Mathews, *Religion and the Old South* (Chicago: University of Chicago Press, 1977) 180-81; and John McCardell, *The Idea of a Southern Nation: Southern Nationalists and Southern Nationalism, 1830-1860* (New York: W. W. Norton & Company, 1979) 200. The best monograph on the divisions in the churches and their effect on the country as a whole is C. C. Goen's *Broken Churches, Broken Nation: Denominational Schisms and the Coming of the Civil War* (Macon GA: Mercer University Press, 1985).

[3]Jerald C. Brauer, "Regionalism and Religion in America," *Church History* 54 (1985): 375-77; Donald M. Scott, *From Office to Profession: The New England Ministry, 1750-1850* (Philadelphia: University of Pennsylvania Press, 1978) 50-51; and Fred J. Hood, *Reformed America: The Middle States, 1783-1837* (University: The University of Alabama Press, 1980) 28-29.

Primarily because of attempts by Northerners to involve themselves in civil matters in the Southern states during the slavery controversy, Southerners formulated a doctrine advocating the strict noninterference of the churches in political affairs. The shock caused by the rise of abolitionism dispelled completely thoughts in any Southerner's mind that a formal synthesis might be formed between public duty and private devotion. The doctrine of the absolute separation of church and state had long been an active part of Baptist tradition in the South, but for Methodists and Presbyterians the adoption of this position represented an important shift in ecclesiastical theory. In order to allow Southerners to manage their secular business without interference from reformers in the North, many Southern evangelicals now argued that the church had no right involving itself with the "things which are Caesar's." The state had a God-given sanction to govern only society, and the church had a similar sanction to superintend only the spiritual sphere.[4]

Presbyterian minister James Henley Thornwell of South Carolina best expressed these ideas when he formulated the concept that became known as "the doctrine of the spirituality of the church." The church is a "spiritual body," Thornwell reasoned, "whose purposes are only the dispensation of eternal salvation, and not the creation of morality, decency and good order, which may . . . be secured without faith in the Redeemer." Too many Americans, he feared, regarded the church as just "a moral institute of universal good, whose business it is to wage war upon every form of human ill." Thornwell conceded that the healthy operation of the church in its own appropriate sphere might affect the general interests of citizens and contribute to the moral progress of humanity, but he denied that the church as an institution ought to be concerned with the promotion of secular well-being. The church, he believed, had "no commission to construct society afresh, to adjust its elements . . . , to rearrange the distribution of its classes, or to change the forms of its political constitutions." In Thornwell's mind, it was theoretically impossible for the Christian faith to have a social relevance, for church and society were "as planets moving in different orbits, . . . each . . . confined to its own track."[5]

---

[4]Anne C. Loveland, *Southern Evangelicals and the Social Order, 1800-1860* (Baton Rouge: Louisiana State University Press, 1980) 202-204; Hill, *South and the North*, 1-12; and Scott, *From Office to Profession*, 110-11.

[5]James Henley Thornwell, *The Collected Writings of James Henley Thornwell, D.D., LL.D.*, ed. John B. Adger and John L. Girardeau (Richmond: Presbyterian Committee of Publication, 1871-1873) 4:449, 469; James Oscar Farmer, Jr., "The Metaphysical Confederacy: James Henley Thornwell and the Synthesis of Southern Values" (Ph.D. diss., University of South Carolina, 1982) 320-22; Kuykendall, *Southern Enterprize*, 165-66; and Loveland, *Southern Evangelicals*, 205.

Social factors also shaped the ways in which churchmen viewed the relationship of religion and culture in America. In the tightly knit, orderly villages of colonial New England, the church held a position that was central to the everyday life of the region and, as a consequence, vigorously upheld a theory that buttressed its already existing civil responsibilities. The Puritans who founded the New England towns had bound themselves together as citizens by covenants that constantly reminded them of their duties and corporate responsibility for the total society. They attempted to create a community in which all citizens would live genuinely ethical lives. However, the growth of towns and cities, the coming of industrialization, and the arrival of significant numbers of foreign immigrants in the first half of the nineteenth century forced Christians in the North to accommodate themselves to changing social conditions. Ethnic and religious pluralism—despite resentment and resistance—became accepted facts of life. These changes, rather than encouraging evangelicals to retreat from social involvement, instead inspired them to participate in ever more vigilant efforts to oversee the moral state of their culture. Opposing religious and political threats that menaced the cultural hegemony enjoyed by evangelical Protestantism, mainline Protestants in the North were convinced that if they withdrew from active engagement in society, those hostile forces might triumph.[6]

In the South, on the other hand, the social position of the church had always been very different from that in the North. Towns had been largely nonexistent in the colonial period, and the population was scattered throughout the countryside. The establishment of Anglicanism in the Southern colonies had been feeble, resisted even by Anglican laymen, and as a result the church had played only a small role in colonial society. Southern evangelicalism, moreover, arose at the end of the eighteenth century, in opposition to the prevailing culture. Methodists, Baptists, and even many Presbyterians were common folk, often poor, and usually cut off from the economic and political concerns of the leaders of the South. Evangelicals quite self-consciously emphasized their low social standing, and neither professed nor showed much interest in maintaining the solidarity of the larger society.[7]

---

[6]Hill, *South and the North*, 76-77; and Mathews, *Religion in the Old South*, 41.

[7]Hill, *South and the North*, 7, 73-75; Mathews, *Religion in the Old South*, 41; Wyatt-Brown, *Southern Honor*, 18-19; and John B. Boles, *The Great Revival, 1787-1805: The Origins of the Southern Evangelical Mind* (Lexington: The University of Kentucky Press, 1972) 170-71.

Despite the emergence of evangelical Protestantism as the religious consensus of the Southern people in the middle of the nineteenth century, its ideology never really outgrew this social heritage. The South became increasingly more unified in its political, cultural, and religious thought as it progressed toward its revolt from the North, yet the ethic that dominated Southern churches remained a private, individualistic one. Although many Southerners assumed that the internal restraints of individuals, when taken collectively, would actually strengthen the social order, churchmen still made their principal appeal to individuals alone. Influential ministers reminded their people that religion was not a thing of this world and was concerned only with souls, not with society. Effective moral reformation was strictly an inner process.[8]

Few Southern Christians directly challenged the fundamental structure and ethos of their society. Yet in some cases, nineteenth-century evangelicals *did* set themselves against popular opinion and upheld points of view on such issues as temperance, Sabbath observance, dueling, and gambling that were sharply critical of vices in which many Southerners supposedly engaged. Even though the church in the South was not radically antagonistic to its culture, it forcefully confronted what it judged to be instances of immoral behavior otherwise acceptable to society as a whole. By condemning individuals for the sins they committed, Southern churchmen implicitly separated themselves from the culture that appeared to condone those sins.[9]

Some clergymen even feared that as a class they had become alienated from the rest of society. John Holt Rice, a leading clerical voice of Southern Presbyterianism, for example, criticized ministers who "meddled" in temporal affairs and thereby revived "the old jealousy" between church and state in the South. The epitaph of Ezekiel Polk in Tennessee is expressive (albeit in a humorous way) of animosity that Rice sensed, and against which many Southern evangelicals struggled. "Here lies the dust of old E. P.," the tombstone reads,

---

[8]E. Brooks Holifield, *The Gentlemen Theologians: American Theology in Southern Culture, 1795-1860* (Durham NC: Duke University Press, 1978) 145-54; and Boles, *Great Revival*, 182.

[9]Wyatt-Brown, *Southern Honor*, 341-43.

One instance of mortality;

• • •

From superstition liv'd quite free,
And practiced [sic] strict morality;
To holy cheats was never willing
To give one solitary shilling;
He can foresee and for foreseeing
He equals most of men in being,
That Church and State will join their pow'r
And mis'ry on this country show'r,
And Methodists with their camp bawling
Will be the cause of this down falling;
      An era not destined to see,
It waits for poor posterity.
First fruits and tithes are odious things,
And so are Bishops, Priests, and Kings.[10]

Clergymen insisted, furthermore, that true religion, rather than being conformed to the world, ought to transform the world in the image of Jesus Christ. By emphasizing that government existed solely by divine ordinance, evangelicals in the South also placed themselves in opposition to familiar nineteenth-century notions of self-reliance and popular democracy. As James Henley Thornwell stated, the legitimate purpose of government was not to do the people's will, but to "enforce what reason, conscience and truth pronounce to be right." The corruption wrought by democratic government, Thornwell and other Southern churchmen believed, was one of the symptoms of a general spiritual declension prevalent in their age. The sovereignty of God required that he govern the world for his own glory and according to his own laws, while the full comprehension of God's actions was beyond human powers altogether.[11]

One must not conclude from the above argument, however, that Thornwell or his disciples thought that the Southern social structure was entirely outside God's providential governance. Nor should one think that Southern

---

[10]Ernest Trice Thompson, *The Spirituality of the Church: A Distinctive Doctrine of the Presbyterian Church in the United States* (Richmond: John Knox Press, 1961) 20-21; and the tombstone of Ezekiel Polk (died 31 August 1804) in the Polk Family Cemetery, Bolivar TN.

[11]Thomas Smyth, "Religion in Politics," *Southern Presbyterian Review* 15 (1863): 587-91; Loveland, *Southern Evangelicals,* 126-27; and Hood, *Reformed America,* 28-29.

evangelicalism absolutely lacked a social ethic. Quite the opposite. Every existing society, even a flawed one, carried a special mandate from God and was assured of a steady progress to a richer maturity prepared for it by God. Thornwell castigated reformers for their bold assumption that they could accelerate the natural, divinely ordained tempo of social progress. Social reform injected a disruptive thrust into the natural harmonies that God had created between church and society. Thornwell wished always to "follow nature," for he believed that society functioned best when left to itself. In a homogeneous society like the South's, moreover, the willingness to accept the social order as it was insured that evangelicalism would always maintain some influence—even if only a negative one—in the larger culture. The theological basis of Thornwell's doctrine of the spirituality of the church, therefore, was not (by its own lights) radically individualistic, but organic and socially cohesive.[12]

In the past, some historians have dismissed Southern evangelicalism as simply a "culture religion," wholly shaped by and subservient to the social ideology of the South. There is truth to this idea, and scholars have rightly questioned whether the doctrine of the spiritual church *actually* meant what it said it did. One scholar, Jack P. Maddex, has argued recently that Southern churchmen were "theocrats" who gave the church a great role in strengthening civil authority. While upholding the separation of church and state in an elementary sense, these clergymen were in fact contriving to bring tremendous pressure upon government to take action on what they considered to be moral issues. Focusing specifically on Southern Presbyterians, Maddex believes that throughout the antebellum period, and at least until 1865, the leaders of this denomination expected that the church could rebuke public officials, condemn immoral policies, and teach their people social duties. Although his case has by no means received universal acceptance, it does provide a coherent explanation for the Presbyterians' activity during the 1850s.[13]

Probably the best general analysis of the differences between the teachings of Northerners and Southerners on ethical matters is Bertram

---

[12]Theodore Dwight Bozeman, "Science, Nature and Society: A New Approach to James Henley Thornwell," *Journal of Presbyterian History* 50 (1972): 319-24; and Hill, *South and the North*, 7, 74.

[13]Loveland, *Southern Evangelicals*, ix-x; Jack P. Maddex, "From Theocracy to Spirituality: The Southern Presbyterian Reversal on Church and State," *Journal of Presbyterian History* 54 (1976): 438-47; and John B. Boles, "Evangelical Protestantism in the Old South: From Religious Dissent to Cultural Dominance," in *Religion in the South*, ed. Charles Reagan Wilson (Jackson: University Press of Mississippi, 1985) 174 n.16.

Wyatt-Brown's collection of essays *Yankee Saints and Southern Sinners*. Throughout this book, Wyatt-Brown depicts men of both regions wrestling with the meaning of the concepts of individualism and communal responsibility for themselves and for their societies on the eve of the Civil War. For some Northerners, the Puritan heritage seemed to have dissolved long ago into romantic individualism; for others, a belief in human perfectibility required that individual actions benefit the community as a whole. Southerners were similarly divided. The paternalism of the slave system envisioned a society that was stable, hierarchical, and preoccupied with relationships within itself. Yet the equally strong tradition of libertarianism in the South prevented the development of strong institutions, and Southerners remained skeptical concerning the possibility and worthwhileness of ameliorating the injustices present in their society. While the evangelical ethic encouraged individuals in the North to undertake reform activities on behalf of society, that same ethic as it existed in the South demanded only conformity to the community will. The individualism that Southern evangelicalism embraced, therefore, was in no way antinomian. But neither was that ethic capable, it seems, of formulating a *positive* ideology of social responsibility.[14]

Irony is inherent in the history of the South, as C. Vann Woodward has persuasively and eloquently argued. Forced to struggle with the experiences of tragedy and defeat in a rich and successful nation, Southerners have seen their history in sharp contrast to that of the North. In *The South and the North in American Religion*, Samuel Hill gives further shape to this idea of Southern distinctiveness by discussing the religious life of the two regions during the nineteenth century. Unfortunately, Hill's discussion omits the Civil War, and although his decision is understandable, given the broad scope of his work, a crucial era in American history has been ignored. The Civil War, I think, demands examination using a scheme similar to Hill's, for religion had a strong impact on the development of cultural ideologies (in the South especially) after 1865, as well as on the war effort of the two armies.[15]

---

[14]Wyatt-Brown, *Yankee Saints and Southern Sinners* (Baton Rouge: Louisiana State University Press, 1985) 9-10, 16, 22, 149, 168, 214-15.

[15]C. Vann Woodward, "The Search for Southern Identity" and "The Irony of Southern History," in C. Vann Woodward, *The Burden of Southern History* (Baton Rouge: Louisiana State University Press, 1960) 3-25, 167-91; and Hill, *South and the North*, 1-12.

The questions that most interest me concern the differences in the relationship of religion and culture in the North and the South, and the
manifestation of those differences within the military forces of the two regions. Specifically, I am proposing that the Southern churches were less
successful in supporting the Confederate war effort, and the Northern
churches more successful in supporting the Union one, than has usually
been assumed.

The highly individualistic religion of the South, with its overriding emphasis on personal salvation, generally failed to serve a proper social function. Rather than strengthening the resolve of the Southern people to support
the struggle for political independence, religion in the South actually undermined the Confederate war effort. I am convinced that twentieth-century
writers such as Allen Tate and James McBride Dabbs were right to censure
religion in their region for its inadequate concern for public needs. In many
a Southern evangelical, furthermore, there were aspects of William Faulkner's character Goodhue Coldfield, who literally walled himself up as a moral
protest against participation in the Civil War. Coldfield withdrew from fighting not because he was a coward, Faulkner's narrator says, but because he
balked at the "idea of waste"—the waste inextricably associated with aiding
any worldly cause. One finds strong, impressionistic suggestions throughout
the writings of the war period that indicate how certain aspects of Southern
religion diminished the willingness of some Southerners to fight once the war
began to turn against them.[16]

Attributing defeat to the failure of Southern morale, of course, is an
idea that is not original with me. In 1960, Charles G. Sellers suggested
that a sense of guilt about slavery produced unease in the Southern people
and tempered their original enthusiasm for secession and war. Kenneth
Stampp also elaborated on this theme in his 1968 essay "The Southern
Road to Appomattox." He stated boldly that "many southerners . . . who
outwardly appeared to support the Confederate cause had inward doubts
about its validity, and that, in all probability, some perhaps uncon-
sciously, welcomed defeat." Stampp linked these doubts specifically to
ambivalence about the moral burdens imposed by slavery, and he concluded that the South was not equipped "not only physically but spiritu-

---

[16]Allen Tate, "Remarks on the Southern Religion," in *I'll Take My Stand: The South
and the Agrarian Tradition* (New York: Harper Torchbooks, 1962) 174-75; James McBride
Dabbs, *Haunted by God* (Richmond: John Knox Press, 1972) 206; William Faulkner, *Absalom, Absalom!* (New York: Vintage Books, 1972) 82-83, 260; and Fred Hobson, *Tell About
the South: The Southern Rage to Explain* (Baton Rouge: Louisiana State University Press,
1983) 345-48.

ally and ideologically as well" for the challenge that the Civil War presented.[17]

More recently, James Oakes's thoughtful, provoking analysis of the thinking of slaveowners in the Old South has discussed the unnerving effects that evangelicalism had upon the psyches of masters who were religious. By rejecting a sinful, covetous world, evangelicalism carried an antimaterialistic message that struck slaveholders with great force and made many of them become guiltridden. Their religious faith told them that what the secular culture valued was actually wrong and sinful, and that any worldly success a man derived from holding other men in bondage could well endanger the state of his soul. This knowledge placed a tremendous emotional burden on masters, Oakes notes, that was relieved only by their frequently expressed desire to be rid of their slaves entirely. Because of the moral ambiguities created by slaveholding, at least a few pious Southerners may have wondered to themselves if losing the war would quiet their religious anxieties and remove the curse of slavery from them. Losing the war, therefore, might bring them the absolution that they desired but could not realistically obtain any other way.[18]

The latest book to address this problem directly is the compelling multiauthor work *Why the South Lost the Civil War*. In it Richard Beringer, Herman Hattaway, Archer Jones, and William Still apply the hypotheses of Sellers, Stampp, and Oakes to questions concerning the causes of Confederate defeat, and they connect the failure of the South's war for independence to the "religious fatalism" of Southern Christianity. Religion and the guilt that it induced among Southern evangelicals made military reverses acceptable and became one of the key reasons for the ultimate surrender of the South. Unlike the North's activistic, reform-minded churchmen, Christians in the South viewed their world with only "an ironic, uneasy satisfaction"—a religious mindset that hindered the effective waging of the revolutionary conflict the Confederacy undertook.[19]

Although most clergy tried to be active supporters of Confederate morale, and although churchgoers were as patriotic as any other group of citizens, a toll had already been exacted upon the hearts and minds of believers

---

[17]Richard E. Beringer, et al., *Why the South Lost the Civil War* (Athens: The University of Georgia Press, 1986) 22, 356-58; and Kenneth Stampp, *The Imperiled Union: Essays on the Background of the Civil War* (New York: Oxford University Press, 1980) 252, 260.

[18]James Oakes, *The Ruling Race: A History of American Slaveholders* (New York: Alfred A. Knopf, 1982) 102-104, 109, 119-22; and Mathews, *Religion in the Old South*, 79-80, 150, 152, 173.

[19]Beringer, *Why the South Lost*, 93-94, 359-62.

in the South. Southern evangelicalism contained a basic internal dilemma so pronounced that it easily may have become a self-fulfilling prophecy of defeat. If the church truly was not concerned with the affairs of the state, and if individuals really were not ethically responsible for their culture, and if the salvation that Christians sought was available solely in the world to come, then religious citizens might be expected to find personal contentment even when confronted by earthly ruin. Since the dominant moral ethic of the South directed Christians to seek little direct engagement with their society, many of them may have been disappointed when their nation failed to win its fight against the Union, but they could hardly have been surprised that the world brought frustrations upon them. Southern evangelicals, after all (as Donald Mathews has observed regarding the slavery controversy), had always known the meaning of defeat.[20]

I also believe that religion played an important role in leading the Northern troops to victory. Although the religious life in the Union armies has often been ignored in standard histories about the war, documentation on that subject is, in fact, plentiful. In the North, church leaders were significantly involved in the struggle, and their spiritual contributions to the Union cause aided Northern morale. Revivalism in the Union forces served as a kind of barometer of the Northern mood. Thus, revivals in the Northern camps gained strength at the same time the triumph of the North became more and more a certainty. Union army revivals inspired the soldiers to redouble their offensive thrusts against the South.[21]

Religion fulfilled quite different needs in the North and the South, and the churches in the two sections consequently played different roles during the war. Most prominent clergy and churchmen in the North thought that their faith made them accountable for society and encouraged them to direct their moral energy toward civic ends. The Northern mainline denominations, as a result, could be effective agencies for encouraging their members to serve in the defense of the Union and to find more than just worldly satisfaction in pressing the North on to military victory. Since Southern religious ideology, on the other hand, emphasized the worth of

---

[20]Mathews, *Religion in the Old South*, 77-78.

[21]Even James H. Moorhead's fine book *American Apocalypse: Yankee Protestants and the Civil War, 1860-1869* (New Haven: Yale University Press, 1978) says comparatively little about how religious activity in the army related to other developments in the Northern churches during that period.

individual moral development and theoretically resisted the notion of Christians' participation in secular affairs, it tended by implication to discourage a full commitment to the sordid work of winning the war. Religion in the South made its most useful contribution to Southern culture only after the war ended, when it emerged as a convincing symbol of the value of spiritual victory in midst of the earthly defeat.

The Ploughshare of War: The Mission to the Union Armies

1

Speaking before the 1865 meeting of the Massachusetts Bible Society, George L. Walker invited its members to rejoice with him at the events that had occurred in America that year. He told them that they should not only feel gladdened at the emergence of the Union as victor in the war, but also well satisfied with the large role played by the Bible in the Northern triumph. Walker cited the English Civil War and the landing of the Pilgrims at Plymouth as other examples of how the Bible was responsible for major strides mankind had made toward civil liberty and political freedom. In the Union army, that book had been put to "a wondrous test," and as a result it could now be read "like a new volume." The Bible had proved to be a "document written in sympathetic ink" that merely needed "the fires of war" and "the light which has shone from our camps" to reveal its true significance to Americans.[1]

The pleasure Walker felt at the results of the Civil War was, of course, typical of spokesmen for the Northern churches. Many of these leaders, in fact, were genuinely surprised that the war had aided the growth and renewal of the churches as much as it had, considering the experience of the churches in the American Revolution, a war that supposedly had proved disastrous to piety both at home and in the army. Although some clergy had at first expected to see only "the moral waste of war—character perverted, and vicious habits acquired—sadder far than any mere loss of life," they soon learned that their worst fears were unwarranted. Instead, they praised the Civil War as a force that revived religion in the North in the 1860s. Northern Protestants especially were delighted to discover that

---

[1]Massachusetts Bible Society, *Annual Report* 56 (1865): 20-21.

the war had actually increased the number of church members in a dramatic fashion, and it had proved a boon to their domestic missionary activities as well.[2]

While Northern clergy watched the steady advance of the Union armies at the end of the war, they marveled at the effects of victory upon their people, as men and women flocked to the churches in the time of crisis. *The Home Missionary*, magazine of the American Home Missionary Society, for example, had earlier noted that young men were being drawn away from the beguiling influence of material interests and back to the responsibilities of religion. Rather than ruining Christian benevolent activity, the excitements of wartime had heightened it and (*The Home Missionary* hoped) would lead soldiers into the demanding life of missionary service when peace came. A writer in the *Methodist Quarterly Review* drew a similar conclusion and expected that general church growth would be a result of the war. "It is a matter for thankfulness that at the North every cause of religious or intellectual progress has greatly prospered" now, wrote L. P. Brocket. Brocket hoped that one day a renewed domestic missionary movement in America would be recognized as the "first fruits of the discipline" of the Civil War.[3]

When *The Monthly Journal of the American Unitarian Association* called the war a glorious day "in which selfishness seems almost to have disappeared," it voiced a common theme among church people in the North. The editor of that journal declared that he was thankful for the war's demonstrating that the North was "not a nation of shopkeepers" who only loved money. Instead, the war again taught Christians the value of self-denial and showed Northerners how to be a country of men and women who were "filled with the desire to make some sacrifice for the good cause." This spirit was viewed by these theological liberals as a spiritual impulse and evidence of a revival of religious interest in America. As Frederic Hedge, president of the American Unitarian Association, announced in 1861, the "self-sacrificing patriotism" inspired by the war was fundamentally "religious in its essence, however unritual in its form."[4]

Allied with this theme was the assumption that the sacrifices of the Civil War were for the sake of a virtuous end that would benefit the nation

---

[2]Richard Howard Ekman, "Northern Religion and the Civil War" (Ph.D. diss., Harvard University, 1972) 154-55; and Elbridge Gerry Brooks, "Our Civil War," *Universalist Quarterly* 17 (1861): 263-64.

[3]*The Home Missionary* 36 (1863-1864): 69-70, 229-31; and L. P. Brocket, "Philanthropy in War Time," *Methodist Quarterly Review* 47 (1865): 77, 80-86.

[4]*The Monthly Journal of the American Unitarian Association* 2 (1861): 228-29, 299.

as well as the churches. Northern clergymen believed that America, purified and reborn in the war, would be better enabled to undertake the grand mission to which God had summoned it: the promotion of political and religious liberty throughout the world. Although clergy before the war had lamented that the United States had strayed from God's original purposes, the war convinced many of them that God had directed the nation back to its intended vocation. In apocalyptic imagery, Julia Ward Howe's "Battle Hymn of the Republic" epitomized this sense of mission and visualized Northern soldiers as actors in the eschatological conflict with the forces of evil. Northern Protestants identified the deaths of their soldiers with the sacrificial death of Jesus Christ and expected that the release of blacks from bondage actually presaged the coming of God's heavenly glory into human history.[5]

The Civil War provided a channel of grace for America, and in death soldiers became bearers of that grace. The willingness to fight and die was seen as an impulse worthy of a Christian martyr; it brought redemption to both the soldier himself and the nation for which he fought. The following two poems published in the Unitarian *Monthly Religious Magazine* exemplify the kind of millennial significance that Northern churchmen envisioned when they described their participation in the war.

"The Home Guard," for instance, celebrated the bravery of citizen-soldiers who went to the field of battle to suppress the Southern rebellion. The author believed that the men gave their lives on behalf of "the dawning age of God." These soldiers were shown to be conscious of the apocalyptic meaning of the war and of their own role as actors in the final drama of salvation.

> *For they break the night of terror,*
> *And drive back the ancient error,*
> *Leading in the day divine.*

---

[5]Robert L. Stanton, *The Church and the Rebellion: A Consideration of the Rebellion . . . and the Agency of the Church, North and South, in Relation Thereto* (Freeport NY: Books for Libraries Press, 1971) vii; Peter J. Parish, "The Instruments of Providence: Slavery, Civil War, and the American Churches," in *The Church and War: Papers Read at the Twenty-First Summer Meeting and the Twenty-Second Winter Meeting of the Ecclesiastical History Society*, ed. W. J. Sheils (Oxford: Basil Blackwell, 1983) 319; Robert Albrecht, "The Theological Response of the Transcendentalists to the Civil War," *New England Quarterly* 38 (1965): 22; Ernest Lee Tuveson, *Redeemer Nation: The Idea of America's Millennial Role* (Chicago: The University of Chicago Press, 1968) 191, 202; and James H. Moorhead, *American Apocalypse: Yankee Protestants and the Civil War, 1860-1869* (New Haven: Yale University Press, 1978) 56-65.

The other poem, addressed to a young clergyman who had enlisted as a private, spoke of the sacrifice that he and many thousands of Christians made by laying their lives on "the altar" of their country. Wearing "sacred armor," they were said to be fighting not for conquest or vainglory, but for the entrance of the "glorious day,"

> *When united peace and freedom*
> *Shall their banner pure display!*
>
> *When throughout [God's] wide dominions,*
> *War and tyrant wrong shall cease;*
> *And the Lord shall reign forever,*
> *King of nations, Prince of Peace.*[6]

This optimistic millenarian spirit provided a powerful set of religious images that even crossed racial lines and appealed as strongly to many Northern black churchmen as to whites. A prominent figure like Frederick Douglass embraced the same myths about America's mission that impelled mainline churchgoers in the war, and he saw a great purpose in the suffering the country was undergoing. Heavenly warriors, Douglass thought, were prosecuting the fight along with Union soldiers, and their presence would insure that the blood shed by Americans would save the nation from its sins. The war was not waged just to liberate Southern blacks, but to free the whole world from oppression by demonic powers. Douglass challenged American men to take their divinely appointed position in the battleline and there to do "a great service for mankind." Those who died in the war might rightly be mourned by friends and loved ones, yet the offering of their lives was so noble and grand that it far transcended any ordinary human sense of sorrow or tragedy.[7]

Some Northerners went so far as to draw an analogy between the deaths of their troops and the atoning act of Christ on Calvary. They visualized Union soldiers as redemptive agents who saved their countrymen from the consequences of the sin of tolerating slavery for so long. "The red right arm of God is achieving . . . redemption," Methodist minister Gilbert Haven told a Boston gathering in 1863. Haven believed that God had poured out "the plague of war and its abounding miseries" because the

---

[6]*The Monthly Religious Magazine* 26 (1861): 119; and ibid., 28 (1862): 292-93. See also Thomas Brainerd, *Remarks of Rev. Dr. Brainerd at the Funeral of Lieut. John T. Greble, U.S.A.* (Philadelphia: G. T. Stockdale, 1861) 5.

[7]David W. Blight, "Frederick Douglass and the American Apocalypse," *Civil War History* 31 (1985): 319-23.

churches had refused to work for the release of those enslaved in the South. Furthermore, Unitarian Cyrus Bartol suggested that the war was an "atonement by blood" for his land. Every Union "martyr" mingled his blood "with that of the great Redeemer of mankind." He thereby insured that his country would survive its ordeal and sublimely rise to receive God's blessing as a reward for its agony.[8]

Other clergymen picked up on the theme of atonement, and none better articulated that idea than Horace Bushnell of Hartford. Bushnell perceived the war as a providential opportunity for Americans to reform themselves as a nation under divine guidance. So momentous a crisis was the Civil War that he was moved to exclaim in a letter, "I thank God that I have been allowed to see this day. . . . Better to have a country worthy of adversity than one that is subject to shame and contempt." Bushnell trusted that the war, despite all the suffering that it entailed, was actually a sign of God's "favoring word and purpose" upon the United States. By fighting in the conflict, Northerners were granted the chance to prove their devotion to true religion, that is, to the Christian principles upon which their nation's government should have been based eighty years before.[9]

The disturbing news of the defeat at First Bull Run inspired Bushnell's most remembered sermon, *Reverses Needed.* In this address, he spoke of the war as a contest for a God-given nationhood. God inflicted reverses upon the North so that Americans might—in apparent misfortune—come to realize that God's hand alone directed the course of national life. Bushnell thought that, although Southerners like Thomas Jefferson had tried to entice Americans into believing that "the people" controlled the national destiny, the war would teach Northerners (and eventually Southerners, too) that God was really the author of all human government. Bushnell condemned the South, therefore, not only for perpetrating the sin of slavery, but also for forcing a false national consciousness on Americans. God had brought the torment of war upon the United States to allow the country the chance to atone for *both* those sins. Peace eventually

---

[8]William Gravely, *Gilbert Haven, Methodist Abolitionist: A Study in Race, Religion, and Reform, 1850-1900* (Nashville: Abingdon Press, 1973) 114; Cyrus Bartol, *The Remission by Blood: A Tribute to Our Soldiers and the Sword, Delivered in the West Church* (Boston: Walker, Wise, and Company, 1862) 4-5, 8-9; and Albrecht, "Theological Response of the Transcendentalists," 28-29.

[9]Mary Bushnell Cheney, *Life and Letters of Horace Bushnell* (New York: Charles Scribner's Sons, 1903) 474; and Howard A. Barnes, "The Idea That Cause a War: Horace Bushnell versus Thomas Jefferson," *Journal of Church and State* 16 (1974): 81.

would come, but without the shedding of blood no divine grace could possibly be granted.[10]

The war caused such immense suffering that not even the victors could escape feeling somewhat subdued by it. Northern clergy pointed accusing fingers at sins that had been fostered by the prosperity of their region and had stirred up God's righteous anger against the North: Sabbath breaking, intemperance, and widespread materialism. Since nations would not be present at the final judgment, they had to receive their punishment from God in the present age. "God has loaded us with benefits," the bishops of the Episcopal Church declared in 1862, "and with our benefits have grown our ingratitude, our self-dependence, and self-sufficiency, our pride, our vain-glorying." Because Americans dared to think that all their material blessings and rewards had been earned by their own hands, God's "chastening Providence" reminded them that human ability had its limits. How "wonderful" were the tribulations that the war brought, then, for in them Northerners could again see that only God ruled the affairs of men.[11]

In the eyes of most mainline Christians in the North, however, the Civil War was not merely punishing the American people; it was purifying them as well for further service as a nation. Preachers usually looked beyond the grim present of military reverses and casualties on the battlefield to view a rosier future for their country. For them, the war was a terrible "discipline" that was conferring the "benefits of a pruning knife," eliminating undesirable elements in the national character and perfecting the American people above all others. "War has ennobled . . . us," Thomas Brainerd, moderator of the General Assembly of the New School Presbyterians, confidently stated. Brainerd predicted that patriotism and piety would aid each other in the wartime crisis. The war would cleanse the Northern churches of whatever sins beset them, and thus purified, those churches could secure by their prayers the blessings of God upon the Union war effort.[12]

---

[10]Horace Bushnell, *Reverses Needed: A Discourse Delivered on the Sunday After the Disaster of Bull Run* (Hartford: L. E. Hunt, 1861) 8-9, 21-23; William A. Clebsch, *Christian Interpretations of the Civil War* (Philadelphia: Fortress Press, 1969) 6-11; and Moorhead, *American Apocalypse*, 139-41.

[11]"Pastoral Letter of the Bishops of the Protestant Episcopal Church in the United States of America Delivered before the General Convention . . . October 17, 1862," in Protestant Episcopal Church in the United States of America, *Journal of the General Convention* (1862): 4-6; and Massachusetts Baptist Convention, *Annual Report* 59 (1861): 11.

[12]Charles Wadsworth, *War a Discipline: A Sermon Preached in Calvary Church, San Francisco* (San Francisco: H. H. Bancroft and Company, 1864) 9, 23; and Thomas Brainerd, *Patriotism Aiding Piety: A Sermon* (Philadelphia: William F. Geddess, 1863) 17-18.

In a similar fashion, George Templeton Strong, a prominent Episcopal layman, spoke about how church and state in the North ought to provide mutual assistance during the war. Strong insisted, in fact, that the
Civil War was fundamentally a "religious war" between two opposing
creeds, locked in a struggle for possession of the continent. Strong was
convinced that Southern Christianity was closer to "Mahometanism" than
to the historic faith of Christendom. Rather than teaching the ethics of
the New Testament, Southerners had made "crime and oppression" and
the debasement of their working class the foundation of their religious
creed. Strong rejoiced that the war had brought together again "Church
and State, Religion and Politics" in a practical venture that would benefit
them both. Although Southerners once had tried to dismiss the church as
a private organization that had no relation to important public affairs, the
war had shown how mistaken that notion was. The sympathies of the
church in the North clearly lay with those of the state, for in prosecuting
the war against the allegedly irreligious South, the government was also
helping the cause of religion. [13]

Gilbert Haven was another churchman who saw in the Civil War a continuation of the antebellum struggle between pious Northerners, who wished
to establish a "Christian democracy" in America, and recalcitrant Southerners. The Northerners' goal could never have been realized if religion had been
relegated to an exclusively private context, but the war had made the Southerners' position no longer tenable. The divorce of morality from politics that
had been made in the national compromise over slavery had produced, Haven said, "a more shameful prostitution of the ministry and the church than
in any country in modern history." Before 1861, churchmen who dared teach
that faith had no connection with social or civil responsibility had won the
day; the war was now clearly demonstrating, however, that their theories were
insubstantial and utterly false. [14]

Northern church and state, indeed, did support each other, and never
more dramatically than when soldiers and missionaries in tandem brought
the war home to the churches in the South. As Thomas Hill, president of
Harvard University, announced to the Massachusetts Bible Society, "the
ploughshare of war" had "turned up new fields, and prepared them for the
reception of the seed of life." Although Hill spoke specifically of the opportunities for Northern missionaries to proselytize newly freed slaves, he

---

[13]George Templeton Strong, *The Diary of George Templeton Strong*, ed. Allan Nevins
and Milton Halsey Thomas (New York: The Macmillan Company, 1952) 3:125-26, 356-
57.

[14]Gravely, *Gilbert Haven*, 112-13.

captured the general mood in the North as areas of Confederate territory first came under United States military control. Union victories had given Northern clergymen the opportunity for which they had always longed: a way to deliver the Yankee gospel to the Southern people.[15]

In a sermon in 1862, Unitarian preacher Edward Everett Hale declared his belief that his government bore a responsibility to introduce Christian civilization into the South. Hale intended to share with the benighted Southern states all the North's possessions and special gifts: "manufacture, commerce, science, art, character, and religion." Since the corrupt leadership of the South had led the rebellion against the United States, the war gave the North a God-given occasion for overthrowing that leadership with its own and gathering all the states of a reunited nation under the rule of Puritan habits and Yankee laws.[16]

Clergymen in the Northern states hoped that the war would also bring about the downfall of the old leaders of the churches in the South and their replacement with men whose preaching and theology were in tune with New England religious principles. Rather than teaching Christianity, the Confederate clergy were said to have abetted the spread of moral degeneracy in their region. But through the agency of war, a vast missionary field had now been laid open, where Northern Christians intended to organize their own churches. By the "Providence of God," church workers from the North had been allowed to enter the South again after the lapse of several decades and to plant there the kind of religion and government that God intended the whole American continent to have. This action represented (to use the language of the New School Presbyterians) an "ecclesiastical and Christian reconstruction"—a mission similar to the political and social reconstruction in which other Northerners were beginning to participate as the war drew to a close.[17]

---

[15]Massachusetts Bible Society, *Annual Report* 56 (1865): 23.

[16]Edward Everett Hale, *The Future Civilization of the South: A Sermon* (Boston: N.p., 1862) 12. See also Douglas C. Stange, "United for Sovereignty and Freedom: Unitarians and the Civil War," *The Proceedings of the Unitarian Universalist Historical Society* 19 (1980-1981): 26-27.

[17]Hunter Dickinson Farish, *The Circuit-Rider Dismounts: A Social History of Southern Methodism, 1865-1900* (New York: Da Capo Press, 1969) 48; and Presbyterian Church in the United States of America (New School), *Minutes of the General Assembly* 14 (1865): 19-21, 24-25, 28. See also American Baptist Home Missionary Society, *Annual Report* 32 (1864): 36; American Home Missionary Society, *Report* 39 (1865): 75, 86, 89-95; *American Missionary* 5 (1861): 241-45; ibid., 7 (1863): 154; ibid., 8 (1864): 27-28, 122-23, 242; and Bible Society of Massachusetts, *Annual Report* 54 (1863): 32-33.

Since the start of the Union occupation of parts of the South, various evangelical societies in the North had sent teachers there with instructions to educate and elevate Southern blacks not only intellectually, but also morally and spiritually. The American Missionary Association was the most prominent of these voluntary organizations, and it set the tone for the entire Northern enterprise in the South. Originally formed in 1846 to protest the alleged complicity of the American Home Missionary Society with Southern slaveholders, the AMA advocated political activity and provided antislavery evangelicals with opportunities for using the gospel as a weapon against slavery. During the war, the leadership of the AMA wanted the legal emancipation of slaves to be just the prelude to their "social emancipation," and it told its agents to guide the freedmen in such a way that the blacks could become "useful to themselves, their families, and their country." The AMA desired the efforts of its members to benefit both church and state, and it assumed that the education of the ex-slaves would strengthen American society, government, and religion at one time.[18]

More than any other Northern denomination, the Methodists looked upon the sectional division in their church with extreme dismay and hoped to facilitate the restoration of ecclesiastical and national unity by extending the constituency of "loyal" Methodism to the South. While Methodist membership and wealth in the North increased dramatically between 1861 and 1865, the fortunes of the Methodist Episcopal Church, South, plummeted, and thus Northerners enjoyed a secure position from which they could influence their Southern brethren. The national government, moreover, maintained a cordial relationship with the Methodist Episcopal Church and gave its own support—financial as well as moral—to church members making inroads into captured Southern territory. The government contributed money to the erection of Methodist churches in the South in exchange for the church's promise to allow those buildings to be used also by the Freedmen's Bureau for schools. In this way, church and state each recognized that the war would unite them in a joint, mutually beneficial venture in the defeated South.[19]

---

[18]Leon F. Litwack, *Been in the Storm So Long: The Aftermath of Slavery* (New York: Alfred A. Knopf, 1979) 477. The best monograph on the American Missionary Association is Joe M. Richardson, *Christian Reconstruction: The American Missionary Association and Southern Blacks, 1861-1890* (Athens: University of Georgia Press, 1986).

[19]Farish, *Circuit-Rider Dismounts*, 34-35, 49, 106-107.

Along with a general concern about the moral growth of their nation and the expansion of the churches during the Civil War, Northern Christians felt a special need to evangelize the men in their armies. For the four-year period of the war, therefore, the armed forces became the primary focus of the missionary thrust of the churches. According to almost all ecclesiastical reports issued at the time, that mission was an extraordinarily successful one. From the outset of the war, the army was recognized as a splendid place to promote religious instruction. Although exotic missions in India and China might once have had a romantic appeal to young men, churchmen reasoned, the Union armies presented far more productive occasions for the harvest of souls. Missionary work in the army was inexpensive to maintain, involved no language barriers, and promised the ready availability of many potential converts in relatively small areas.[20]

The need to preserve Christians from the potentially demoralizing influences of army life was also advanced as an important justification for missionary activity. A correspondent to *The Home Missionary*, for example, expressed his fear that many men returning after the war might bear the scars of battle and the "moral scars" received from impure conduct in the camp. Other church members spoke of the acute peril for soldiers who had fallen away from their former beliefs, or had been prey to temptations of the flesh one night, only to be killed in battle the next day. The souls of such men had to be guarded, lest the sins they committed in camp condemn them to suffer for eternity in hell. Since young men assembled in large groups were apt to lead one another into mischief, only the beneficial teachings of religion could check the corrupting forces in those associations.[21]

Most churchmen recognized the Civil War as an opportunity for evangelism that they were not likely to see again. In 1861, Samuel Walley, the president of the Bible Society of Massachusetts, asked those present at the annual meeting if they would dare neglect the souls of the soldiers of their nation. Since so much effort was being expended in caring for the soldiers' bodies, he pointed out, surely the church would wish to give at least equal attention to their souls. "Shall we provide for the *casket*," Walley asked, "and take no thought for the *jewel* which it contains?" The churches were determined to act quickly for the sake of those facing death in battle by

---

[20]Lemuel Moss, *Annals of the United States Christian Commission* (Philadelphia: J. B. Lippincott & Co., 1868) 81-82, 167-68, 202, 208-209.

[21]*The Home Missionary* 35 (1862-1863): 66; T. P. Doggett, "Home Duties in Time of War," *The Monthly Religious Magazine* 30 (1863): 336-37; and Robert Davidson, "Piety Compatible with the Military Life," *The National Preacher* (New Series) 5 (1862): 300.

sending Bibles, tracts, and preachers to tell of the future joys prepared for those who accepted Christ.[22]

However, this resolve confirmed that a notable change had occurred in American evangelicals. Prior to the 1850s, men who served in the army had been held in very low esteem among English-speaking Protestants. They were considered so beneath contempt and such licentious, immoral rabble that their souls were hardly thought to merit saving. But by the mid-nineteenth century, churchmen for the first time recognized the value of a "Christian" army as an effective fighting force. Catherine Marsh's lively biography of Captain Hedley Vicars of the 97th British regiment and John Marshman's memoirs of Major General Henry Havelock were pivotal in this change, for those books contradicted the widely held view that "in making a good Christian you may spoil a good soldier." They presented the then novel idea that there was already a godly minority in that alleged sink of iniquity, the British army, and that there were also many other soldiers who could and should be converted. This thinking inspired evangelicals on both sides of the Atlantic, who thereafter began to look on their armies as seedbeds for religion, ready for missionaries to till.[23]

Taking strength from the lessons of evangelical warriors like Havelock and Vicars, and arguing that religious soldiers actually made the most efficient military men, Northern clergy appealed to secular authorities who otherwise might not welcome them into the army. Patriotic fervor, Christian commitment, and pastoral concern, they said, all seemed to demand that the army mission be given the highest possible priority. Indeed, religion could aid the war effort as much as the war would benefit the cause of religion in America. In an article on "Christian Courage in the Soldier," *The Monthly Religious Magazine* made a straightforward argument for the superiority of religious troops as fighting men. The writer of the article thought that it was faith (along with "mere physical temperament") that raised men above the fear of death and inspired in them "the manhood that makes the soldier truly brave." The author elaborated on how the war had illustrated the truth of what he said, and he hoped that the churches would do all they could to encourage further piety in the Union forces.

---

[22]Bible Society of Massachusetts, *Annual Report* 52 (1861): 12.

[23][Catherine Marsh], *Memorials of Captain Hedley Vicars, Ninety-Seventh Regiment* (New York: Protestant Episcopal Society for the Promotion of Evangelical Knowledge, 1857) viii-ix; John Marshman, *Memoirs of Major-General Sir Henry Havelock, K.C.B.*, 2nd ed. (London: Longman, Green, Longman, and Roberts, 1861) passim; and Olive Anderson, "The Growth of Christian Militarism in Mid-Victorian England," *English Historical Review* 86 (1971): 46-49, 51-52, 60-61, 70-71.

"While those who in peace were least to be depended on are the skulkers and deserters" in wartime, he asserted, the heroic behavior of church members in battle was irrefutable proof that "the best Christians are the best soldiers."[24]

In response to articles like this one in the religious press, and as a result of the belief that there were really too few chaplains to be able to evangelize the soldiers with sufficient vigor, Northern civilians stepped forward to offer aid to their troops. All the denominations, of course, issued appropriate statements about the need for patriotism and the value of fostering morality in the camps. Since military triumph seemed to be both the evidence for and the outcome of God's blessing upon the North, church members gladly showed their gratitude for it. Despite the absence of large numbers of men away in the army, the fund raising and missionary efforts of the churches were not curtailed at all. Benevolent activity still remained strong, and over the course of the war Northerners contributed an estimated $212,000,000 to various war-related charities.[25]

The most enduring and visible contribution made by Northern churchmen to their nation's war effort was the organization of two large institutions that channeled the benevolence of the individual churches. One, the United States Christian Commission, was founded by Protestant evangelicals with the intent of winning the soldiers' souls to Christ. The other, the United States Sanitary Commission, had among its leadership members of the more liberal denominations who viewed their charitable work as essentially religious in nature. The existence of these commissions, and the willingness of the Union government to support the enthusiasm of the men and women who worked in them, reveals the strength of the bonds between church and state in the North throughout the war.

---

[24]The Monthly Religious Magazine 29 (1863): 171-72. Some studies of Civil War deserters had revealed that, in fact, there may have been a correlation between alienation from military authority and hostility to organized religion—deserters usually not being religious men; see Ekman, "Northern Religion and the Civil War," 67.

[25]Moorhead, American Apocalypse, 68-71; Ekman, "Northern Religion and the Civil War," 155, 230-37; William Warren Sweet, The Story of Religions in America (New York: Harper & Brothers, 1930) 467; William Warren Sweet, The Methodist Episcopal Church and the Civil War (Cincinnati: Methodist Book Concern Press, 1912) 138-39, 189-96; Lewis G. Vander Velde, The Presbyterian Churches and the Federal Union, 1861-1869 (Cambridge MA: Harvard University Press, 1932) 429-31; Stange, "United for Sovereignty and Freedom," 18,20; and Charles Richard Denton, "American Unitarians, 1830-1865: A Study of Religious Opinion on War, Slavery, and the Union" (Ph.D. diss., Michigan State University, 1969) 181.

The United States Sanitary Commission was the largest, strongest, and most tightly organized philanthropic body that America had ever seen. It was formed in June 1861 under the direction of Henry W. Bellows, a prominent Unitarian minister in New York City, and saw as its principal mission the dispatching of inspectors to the army to oversee medical care at the front. Bellows had grandiose schemes for the development of the Commission; he wanted it to work according to a plan "based on the best

Front of the United States Sanitary Commission depot, Fredericksburg, Virginia, May 1864 (photograph courtesy of the Library of Congress).

study, the most devoted analysis of the facts, the most cautious and anxious regard to the laws of human nature." Bellows and other members of
his commission originally expected that their organization would function
in a self-consciously elitist role, advising the government on sanitary matters, but shunning direct involvement with the troops. Employing salaried
agents and disdaining so-called sentimental notions of philanthropy, these
leaders were dedicated to the cause of systematic, scientific, and imper-
sonal charity. Ultimately, however, the War Department not only accepted the position of the Commission with the Union forces, but also
depended on it to increase the regular supplies and improve the methods
of the army's own Medical Bureau. Thus, by the end of the war, and even
in spite of the intentions of its founders, the Sanitary Commission had become involved in all aspects of practical aid to the soldiers.[26]

The work of the United States Christian Commission, on the other
hand, manifested the fullest realization of popular evangelical benevolence in the wartime North. Early in the fall of 1861, the New York Young
Men's Christian Association called upon other evangelical organizations
to establish a single national agency to minister to the spiritual needs of
the Union soldiers. A conference in November formed the Christian
Commission and elected as its first president George H. Stuart, a Philadelphia merchant and Presbyterian lay leader. The Commission's leaders
clearly had high expectations concerning the work they wanted to see
done. As an Executive Committee resolution declared in 1864, they believed that there was no "more interesting and important field for missionary operations . . . to be found in the world" than the Union army
camp. The Christian Commission soon became a vast interdenominational fellowship, supporting a hierarchical structure that reached from its
executive committee to field superintendents of the army corps, and then
to more than 5,000 volunteer delegates who were stationed throughout
the Union armies.[27]

[26]William Quentin Maxwell, *Lincoln's Fifth Wheel: The Political History of the United
States Sanitary Commission* (New York: Longmans, Green, 1956) 1-13; Moorhead, *American Apocalypse,* 66-67; George M. Fredrickson, *The Inner Civil War: Northern Intellectuals
and the Crisis of the Union* (New York: Harper & Row, 1968) 98-111; and Robert Lester
Reynolds, "Benevolence on the Home Front in Massachusetts during the Civil War" (Ph.D.
diss., Boston University, 1970) 201.

[27]Moorhead, *American Apocalypse,* 65; Joseph O. Henry, "The United States Christian Commission in the Civil War," *Civil War History* 6 (1960): 374-77; Moss, *Annals,*
602-38; and Minutes of the Executive Committee (14 April 1864) in the United States
Christian Commission Records, Record Group 94, no. 753, National Archives, Washington DC.

The work of the Christian Commission in the field was of two kinds. Initially, delegates helped regimental chaplains bring the Gospel to the soldiers through leadership in worship services, distribution of religious literature, and participation in the pastoral care of the men. Increasingly, though, delegates also ministered to the physical needs of soldiers. Christian Commission workers were especially useful as nurses to soldiers on battlefields and in hospitals. Clergy and laity who went to the armies were delighted to assist surgeons and to learn what they considered to be lessons about "practical" Christianity. Washington Gladden, a leading figure in

Nurses and officers of the United States Sanitary Commission in the backyard of the Sanitary Commission depot, Fredericksburg, Virginia, May 1864 (photograph courtesy of the Library of Congress).

Office of the United States Christian Commission, Washington, D.C. (photograph courtesy of the Library of Congress).

the Social Gospel movement at the end of the century, served briefly as a Christian Commission agent and discovered that ministry involved far more than just the accumulation of theological knowledge. Gladden believed that his army experience had showed him how Christianity involved the commitment of all of one's energies on behalf of his fellow man. As George Stuart replied to those who wanted the Christian Commission to leave temporal matters entirely to the Sanitary Commission, "there is a good deal of religion in a warm shirt and a good beefsteak."[28]

Stuart's remark, however, hints at the hostility that was expressed by members of each commission against the work of the other organization. Since the practical work that they both performed was similar, competition between them was understandable. And since they represented the two rival theological wings of American Protestantism—evangelical and liberal—tensions also were inevitable. In December 1862, the two groups agreed to cooperate, and representatives met in February and April of the next year to work out a plan of mutual assistance. Those who represented the Sanitary Commission considered their rivals hopelessly naive and disorganized. Uncomfortable with the religious beliefs of the "Christians," George Templeton Strong of the Sanitary Commission labeled George Stuart an "evangelical mountebank" and decried the "shallowness, fussiness, and humbug" of his faith. While delegates of the Christian Commisson boasted that their mission was the most exalted, because they came to save the immortal souls of dying men, members of the Sanitary Commission replied that it was more important to save lives and leave souls in God's hands.[29]

The work of the Christian Commission fared much better in the opinion of the United States government than it did in the eyes of the Sanitary Commission leaders. From the outset of the war, Stuart and other members of his executive committee understood the need for official approval and duly received it from President Lincoln, Secretary of War Stanton, and other government members. The government in Washington expressed interest in the religious condition of its troops and attempted to supply Christian Commission agents with support whenever it was feasi-

---

[28]Henry, "United States Christian Commission," 382-83; Moss Annals, 575-76; Washington Gladden, Recollections (Boston: Houghton Mifflin Company, 1909) 140-41; and George H. Stuart, The Life of George H. Stuart, ed. Robert Ellis Thompson (Philadelphia: J. M. Stoddart & Co., 1890) 129.

[29]Maxwell, Lincoln's Fifth Wheel, 191-93, 306; Strong, Diary, 3:310-11, 589; and John Haynes Holmes, The Life and Letters of Robert Collyer, 1823-1912 (New York: Dodd, Mead, and Company, 1917) 1:271-72.

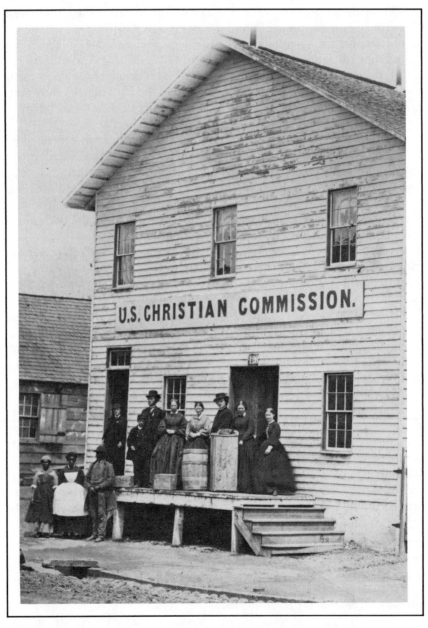

United States Christian Commission depot (photograph courtesy of the Library of Congress).

ble. Although some army officers at first wondered whether every missionary was truly worthy of his high calling (some, they feared, were simply
"curiosity seekers"), acceptance of the Commission was usually polite, if
not always enthusiastic.[30]

As the military fortunes of the North gradually began to improve, the
Christian Commission came to earn more widespread acceptance in the
army. When U.S. Grant assumed overall command of the Union forces

*Supply tents of the United States Christian Commission at the Union encamp-
ment near Germantown, Virginia, in 1863* (photograph courtesy of the Library of Congress).

---

[30]Henry, "United States Christian Commission," 375-76; Moss, *Annals*, 175-76; United
States Christian Commission, *Address of the Christian Commission* (New York: Office of the
Christian Commission, 1862) passim; Marsena Rudolf Patrick, *Inside Lincoln's Army: The
Diary of Marsena Rudolf Patrick, Provost Marshal General, Army of the Potomac*, ed. David
S. Sparks (New York: Thomas Yoseloff, 1964) 271, 448, 475; and Stuart, *Life,* 133.

in the western theater, he ordered that Commission delegates should have free and unhindered access to his troops. Since this order coincided with an intense revival among Northern soldiers at the time of the Chattanooga campaign, Grant was probably aware of the effect of the revivals in strengthening the confidence of his units, and he understood well the need for positive gestures to boost further the morale of his army. After the fall of 1863, and especially after Grant became general-in-chief of all the Union forces, commission agents in every theater of the war found an almost universal reception by Federal officers and men.[31]

The diaries of several delegates working with the armies in Virginia in the last year of the war describe the cordial relations existing between mil-

STATION AT GENERAL HOSPITAL, CITY POINT, VA.

Illustration of both the spiritual and practical ministrations that the United States Christian Commission offered to Northern soldiers (Moss, Annals, 420-21).

[31]Moss, *Annals*, 375-76; and Stuart, *Life*, 133.

itary officials and themselves. Although there is, naturally, a certain amount of self-promotion in these documents, they all speak with *such* enthusiasm for the work that it is hard to gainsay the confidence they expressed. An agent in the 9th Corps, for instance, told of "attentive and eager listeners" who flocked to hear him, the "good respect . . . and appreciation" he received, and the "wide field of usefulness" for clergy in the Christian Commission. A 5th Corps delegate noted that the commander of the 91st Pennsylvania Regiment reproved a soldier who had refused a New Testament that was offered him. This officer's example insured that the members of the regiment, even those who were gambling, politely accepted other offers of Bibles. In fact, the demand for "Testaments" in the 209th Pennsylvania was great enough to exhaust the supply of the Christian Commission worker there and caused him to be criticized for having given too many Bibles away! But "if the Christian Commission cannot give the Word of God freely to all that want it," the agent retorted, "we had better at once . . . strike a bee line for home"[32]

By 1865, the leaders of the mainline denominations in the North had every reason to feel satisfied with what had happened in the war. They were happy, of course, that their country was about to force the Southern armies to surrender. This satisfaction, however, extended far beyond mere chauvinistic exhilaration, for the conflict also seemed to demonstrate conclusively the value of their involvement with their society. Clergymen believed not only that their church members had been morally regenerated by the war, but also that the churches' cooperation with the government had been essential to fostering a religious spirit among the Northern troops. The triumph of the Union had even opened up the South as a new field of evangelism for them, and churchmen hoped that they would be able to return that favor to their government by creating a new class of Union-loving Christians in the Southern states. The war convinced most church members in the North that a supportive relationship could exist between religion and culture in America, and it made them think that those spheres would continue to aid each other as effectively in peace as in war.

---

[32]Diaries of Christian Commission officials (9th Corps, 20 September 1864-21 March 1865; 5th Corps, 20 September 1864-24 March 1865; 18th Corps, 20 September 1864-19 May 1865; Nelson Station, Warrenton Junction VA, 5 February-24 April 1865; and Wild's Station VA, 10 January-24 March 1865) in the Christian Commission Records, Record Group 94, no. 757, Washington DC.

A Call to Repentance, Faith, and Prayer: Southern Denominations and the Confederate Army Camp

2

No major Southern clergyman saw more religious meaning in the Civil War than Presbyterian Benjamin Morgan Palmer of New Orleans. In an 1861 address to the Washington Artillery of his city, he proclaimed that the approaching war between North and South would be "holier" than any conflict that had ever taken place. Southern soldiers were about to go to war to protect religion and civilization against the incursions of the godless Northern hordes. The Washington Artillery, Palmer thought, stood for "a holy cause," and the men of that unit would be able to give their lives in an unequaled act of "martyrdom." On another occasion two years later, Palmer told the South Carolina General Assembly that the war's "preeminent grandeur" lay in the fact that it centered upon "a religious idea." On the one hand, the "wicked infidelity" of the North struck blows of rebellion against the sovereignty of God; on the other hand, the "humble loyalty" of the South received those blows to shield God's sacred majesty. In "the fearful baptism of blood" that the Confederacy was undergoing, Palmer saw patriotism "sanctified by religion," for Southern patriots had accepted a unique opportunity to defend not only their homeland, but the Christian faith as well.[1]

During the war, Southern preachers praised the religious foundations of prerevolutionary America, but they chastised Northerners for straying

---

[1]Thomas Cary Johnson, *The Life and Letters of Benjamin Morgan Palmer* (Richmond: Presbyterian Committee of Publication, 1906) 238-39; and Benjamin Morgan Palmer, *A Discourse Before the General Assembly of South Carolina, on December 10, 1863* (Columbia SC: C. P. Pelham, 1864) 22-23.

from these spiritual roots. America had fallen from its earlier moral purity, Southerners believed, when the founding fathers of the United States introduced the evils of deism and infidelity into the political documents of the new nation. Christians did not fail to note that one of the few differences between the Confederate constitution and that of the United States was the invocation of "Almighty God" in the Southern document. Since God had been restored to his proper place by the elected Confederate officials, clergy were exultant and expected that God would reward the Confederacy for this apparent piety. Like the "return of the prodigal to the bosom of his father," they said, the South had drawn away from the "perilous atheism" that the North had tried to make it practice. "At length, the nation has a God," Benjamin Palmer rejoiced, "Alleluia!"[2]

Agreeing with Palmer's sentiments, many clergymen in the South thought that they were giving a witness to the Christian faith by supporting the political rebellion of their states against Federal authority, and they were at first enthusiastic advocates of secession and the fight for independence. From the beginning of the war, most of the South's churches ostensibly promoted the cause of the Confederacy, and ministers provided whatever assistance they could to aid their country. Claiming that Christians should thrive on the sacrifices that wartime demanded, churchmen gave their all—materially as well as theologically—to supporting their new nation. As James W. Silver's fine study of the churches suggests, ecclesiastical "propaganda" had a significant impact on how the Southern people viewed the war, and the clergy as a group certainly were self-conscious boosters of Confederate morale both at home and at the front.[3]

Yet Silver's book does not tell the full story about the relationship of religion and Southern society. Despite the strength of clerical support for the Confederacy, the ideological presuppositions on which the cooperation was based would eventually undermine the patriotic contributions these churchmen made. In fact, the ministers' vigorous praise of what the Confederacy was accomplishing seemed to imply that their patriotism was in some way conditional and only related to the willingness of the South-

---

[2]Richard T. Hughes, "A Civic Theology for the South: The Case of Benjamin Morgan Palmer," *Journal of Church and State* 25 (1983): 454-55: Carl N. Degler, *Place Over Time: The Continuity of Southern Distinctiveness* (Baton Rouge: Louisiana State University Press, 1977) 99-100; and Robert Manson Myers, ed., *The Children of Pride: A True Story of Georgia and the Civil War* (New Haven: Yale University Press, 1972) 725-26, 855.

[3]Emory M. Thomas, *The Confederate Nation, 1861-1865* (New York: Harper & Row Publishers, 1979) 245-46; and James W. Silver, *Confederate Morale and Church Propaganda* (New York: W. W. Norton & Co., 1967) passim.

ern people to adhere to the laws of God. Clergy wanted their congregations to know that their enthusiasm for the Confederate war effort was predicated not on mindless chauvinism, but rather on the fact that the South stood for true religious principles.

As if recoiling from the enthusiasm of some clergymen in accepting a novel union of church and state, other ministers tempered this ardor by soberly reminding their colleagues that those two spheres should remain just as distinct as they had been before the war. When Presbyterian Thomas Smyth discussed the proper basis for cooperation between religion and politics, for instance, he acknowledged that the situation in the South had changed dramatically in 1861 and that Southern Christians now saw more clearly than before how the temporal and eternal might always have to be related in *this* world. Yet even while making this admission, he added so many caveats to his argument that he robbed it of much of its intended impact. Thus, he lambasted those who wished to involve religion with demagoguery or "unholy principles." He condemned ministers who seeemed too concerned with political squabbling, military posturing, or "worldly affairs" in general. And he insisted that the duty of religion was not to be conformed to the world, but to transform it. The church, Smyth said, was wholly and exclusively a divine institution, based on heavenly rather than earthly foundations, and expounded biblical rather than popular opinion. Since the church should only be interested in the things of God, there could be "no consistent fellowship" between it and the world. No matter how much the Confederate government might honor God, therefore, the sovereignty of God and the independence of the church from the state, Smyth assumed, should still have been the principal concerns of Christian men and women in the South. [4]

James Henley Thornwell also continued his strong advocacy of a "spiritual" church even after the secession of South Carolina, and many patriotic sermons by Southern clergy made that position appear somewhat outdated. Thornwell himself was convinced, of course, that the Confederate cause was a righteous one. But he reminded his fellow church members that the sphere of the church should continue to transcend politics. He defended slavery and the Southerners' war in defense of it, but he asserted at the same time that the church had no scriptural warrant for involving itself with any particular form of government. Although Thornwell thought that Confederate victory would forever protect the churches in the South from interference by Northerners, he placed himself in the par-

---

[4]Thomas Smyth, "Religion and Politics," *Southern Presbyterian Review* 15 (1863): 584-91.

adoxical position of calling Christians to war in order to institute a government that he believed should not—in theory—be concerned with religious matters.[5]

Of all the denominations in the South, Thornwell's Presbyterians had an especially difficult time deciding how they might best support the Confederacy. Ordinary patriotism demanded that they declare their unqualified backing of their new government, yet their sincere theological scruples prevented them from doing that. As a consequence, they had to take halfway measures that, while satisfying the letter of those religious and patriotic requirements, made them appear fainthearted in the effort. When the Synod of South Carolina adopted a motion that supported the defense of its state and nation, it stipulated that this legislative action was undertaken by the churchmen "in their private capacity as a convention of Christian gentlemen," not "in their ecclesiastical capacity as a court of Jesus Christ." Even this somewhat lukewarm resolution, moreover, was removed from the denomination's records by the General Assembly the next year; the General Assembly believed that Presbyterians should appear to be upholding the doctrine of the spirituality of the church with the fullest possible rigor. Although after the war an article in the *Southern Presbyterian Review* explained that political questions were seldom raised in the churches, because the unanimity of the Southern people had simply been *assumed,* the tone of that article also suggested that the churches (Presbyterian and others) did not do all they could have for the Confederate cause. Only once had the article's author heard a political question raised in a church during the war, but that—he was glad to say—had been by "a minister who had lived much in the North!"[6]

Spiritual issues were at stake in the war, and the struggle for political freedom, some churchmen hoped, would increase the Southerners' dependence on God. Church members could express pleasure at the progress that their forces made early in the war. The impulse that led men forth to defend their homes and face death in battle was (in the words of a writer of religious tracts) "heaven-born" and a "sublime gift of God." Amid the

---

[5]Anson Phelps Stokes, *Church and State in the United States* (New York: Harper and Brothers, 1950) 2:236-41; and Benjamin Morgan Palmer, *The Life and Letters of James Henley Thornwell, D.D., LL.D.* (Richmond: Whittet & Shepperson, 1875) 582-88.

[6]James Oscar Farmer, Jr., "The Metaphysical Confederacy: James Henley Thornwell and the Synthesis of Southern Values" (Ph.D. diss., University of South Carolina, 1982) 404-405; and B. T. W., "The Church and Politics," *Southern Presbyterian Review* 18 (1867): 384-88. Farmer, it should be noted, draws a conclusion opposite to mine about the actions of Thornwell and his denomination.

trials that Southern soldiers and civilians were about to endure, God in his mysterious way would bring good out of the evils of wartime. This optimistic view, though, did not last long, for as the first successes of the Confederate armies faded from view, Southerners were confronted all too quickly with the inevitability of defeat. Leaders in the Northern churches remained self-confident throughout most of the war and emphasized that Union soldiers were human agents who brought to fulfillment God's plan for America. Southern churchmen, on the other hand, found few genuine opportunities to be optimistic about either what their soldiers were accomplishing or the outcome of the conflict.[7]

True to the traditions of Reformed theology that nurtured so many Christians in the South, clergymen believed that every military victory their armies won was a result of God's bestowing his favor on those who kept his laws. When Thomas Smyth analyzed the first "glorious victory" that the Confederate forces had gained at Manassas in 1861, he used the opportunity not only to express the glee of the Southern people at turning back the Union invasion of their soil, but also to teach a moral lesson about the need for an army to depend solely on God for help in battle. The truest and best soldiers, he thought, were religious ones. What should the South learn from its experience at First Manassas? That Southerners were better soldiers than Northerners? That Southern society was uniquely righteous? Not at all, said Smyth. God, not the Confederates, had caused the panic of the Union forces and scattered them "as when of old he scattered the Assyrians and Midianites." The Southern triumph in Virginia was not really a blessing; it (along with the entire war) was part of God's "just judgment upon our ungodly land." Smyth hoped that the principle results of the war would be

> a call to repentance, faith, and prayer; . . . a test of religious principle and moral fortitude; . . . a development of Southern national unity; . . . a baptism of blood for the consecration of this new Republic; and . . . a means of reformation of manners, and revival of religion.[8]

Church spokesmen continually interpreted the war in this way and always tried to see military events in the context of God's eternal purposes.

---

[7]Mrs. L. N. B. (of Macon GA), *The Christian Soldier the True Hero: Respectfully Dedicated to the Soldiers of the Confederate States* (Charleston: South Carolina Tract Society [186-]) 1-2; and *Richmond Christian Advocate* 20 (1 May 1862): 2.

[8]Thomas Smyth, "The Victory of Manassas Plain," *Southern Presbyterian Review* 14 (1862): 593, 611-12, 616. For a similar perspective, see also Joseph M. Atkinson, *God, the Giver of Victory and Peace: A Thanksgiving Sermon* ([Raleigh NC]: N.p., 1862) passim.

For a while, religious faith may actually have strengthened the morale of some Southerners and enabled them to look on military defeats as disguised blessings—means by which God purified a chosen people. Such early optimism, however, did not survive for long. As Confederate defeat became more certain each day, churchmen were forced to acknowledge that the war had to be an expression of God's wrath and his judgment against an unfaithful nation. Since evangelicals had warned their people in the antebellum period that their sinfulness invited divine retribution, the Civil War seemed to be an unmistakable indication of how far they had departed from the paths of righteousness. Religion, once a support, now sapped Confederate morale. Defeat, then, did not take Southern evangelicals completely by surprise; in their eyes, their country and fellow citizens were receiving exactly the punishment they deserved.[9]

During the first year and a half of the war, churchmen had trusted that the conflict would bring about "the alienation of the hearts of the people from sin and worldiness, and a return . . . to true contrition for offenses." But when the Southern people seemed no more capable of attaining true repentance than of winning final victory, Christians felt compelled to ask themselves whether God might really have deserted them. Originally Southerners believed that God favored the South, but the ravaging of their land made them wonder why God would allow their enemies to triumph. Typical of the dilemma that white Protestants faced was a resolution debated by a Baptist association in Alabama. A committee proposed that the 1862 meeting should state its belief that "the present civil war which has been inaugurated by our enemies must be regarded as a providential visitation upon us on account of our sins." The majority of the association accepted the substance of that proposal, despite modifying it with the insertion of the phrase "though entirely just on our part." This assumption of the righteousness of the Southern cause notwithstanding, doubts had begun to appear. Christians were starting to realize that God's plans might, in fact, be running exactly opposite to the purposes of the Confederacy.[10]

Sermons by Stephen Elliott, the Episcopal bishop of Georgia, reveal how thoughts in the churches evolved as the true nature of the Civil War gradually became clear. Elliott's tone changed noticeably between 1861

---

[9]Anne C. Loveland, *Southern Evangelicals and the Social Order, 1800-1860* (Baton Rouge: Louisiana State University Press, 1980) 128-29; and Richard E. Beringer, et al., *Why the South Lost the Civil War* (Athens: University of Georgia Press, 1986) 126.

[10]Samuel S. Hill, ed., *Religion in the Southern States: A Historical Survey* (Macon GA: Mercer University Press, 1983) 14; Myers, *Children of Pride*, 993; and Willard E. Wight, "Churches in the Confederacy" (Ph.D. diss., Emory University, 1958) 45-47.

and 1863. In November 1861, for example, Elliott spoke with hopefulness about what the Southern armies were accomplishing in the field. He saw a "high moral tone" in the camp that—in combination with the spiritual aid of the people back home—would make the Confederate forces as unbeatable as Cromwell's Puritan army. A few months later, though, Elliott took a more cautious stance. In February 1862, he worried that the war might not yet have shaken Southern society, which was then "stagnating under the effects of indolence and isolation." Rather than viewing what was happening to the South as only a blessing, he admitted that "war is a fearful scourge," but he prayed that it might still be a "crucible" out of which a holy and noble nation might emerge. By August 1863, Elliott felt called to reassure his listeners that God both disciplines and rewards those whom he has chosen as his people. The goodness of God, he thought, provided security in the face of calamities and tribulations, for through hardship God invariably accomplished his will. Southerners had to trust that the providence of God ultimately would bring good out of the evils they were suffering; that, after all, was the lesson of Calvary.[11]

Elliott saw the results of the Civil War as a beneficial chastisement dealt upon the South by a loving God. No Southern preacher dared concede at the time, of course, that what had happened to the South was desirable in and of itself. But a Christian interpretation like Elliott's enabled church members to accept defeat graciously and look for satisfaction in something else—not merely in winning. Although God had not given the South what Southerners had hoped for, this judgment was a manifestation—however "mysterious and severe"—of his blessings. "We may rejoice through it all," Elliott concluded in 1865, because "nothing can separate us from a love which could give its only-begotten Son for our redemption."[12]

At the latter stages of the war, church members found themselves relying more and more on the expectation that God would intervene miraculously on their behalf. When the war ended and the failure of the Confederacy was certain, most Southern Christians thought defeat was ir-

---

[11]Stephen Elliott, *How to Renew Our National Strength: A Sermon Preached in Christ Church, Savannah, on Friday, November 15th, 1861* (Savannah: John M. Cooper & Co., 1861) 15-16; Stephen Elliot, *"New Wine Not to Be Put Into Old Bottles": A Sermon Preached in Christ Church, Savannah, on Friday, February 28th, 1862* (Savannah: John M. Cooper & Co., 1862) 17-18; and Stephen Elliott, *Ezra's Dilemna* [sic]: *A Sermon Preached in Christ Church, Savannah, on Friday, August 21st, 1863* (Savannah: George N. Nichols, 1863) 8, 16-17, 22-23.

[12]William A. Clebsch, "Baptism of Blood: A Study of Christian Contributions to the Interpretation of the Civil War in American History" (Th.D. diss., Union Theological Seminary, New York, 1957) 185-87.

refutable proof that divine intervention must lie entirely beyond history. Although postmillennialism had been present in the Southern churches prior to 1860, the collapse of the Old South and its social system assured the complete dominance of premillennialism from then on. The sorrows Southerners experienced in the war compelled them to reject forever whatever notions they may once have had about the capacity of human beings to perfect their world. Clergymen cautioned their people to be both patient in the midst of trouble and hopeful of Christ's eventual return to redeem them from their afflictions. Therefore, premillennialism further discouraged Southerners from making a full psychological commitment to the war.[13]

Southern evangelicals, who were already doubtful about the value of involvement in secular affairs, interpreted defeat as an undeniable sign of the futility of placing hopes in worldly institutions. A poem composed by John L. Girardeau captures the sense of the utter despondency present in the churches at the end of the war, and it reflects the premillenialist idea that only Christ's Second Coming would bring relief. Girardeau entreated,

> For thy appearance all things pray
> All nature sighs at thy delay,
> The people cry "no longer stay,"
>   Lord Jesus quickly come!!
>
> Hush the fierce blast of War's alarms
> The tocsins toll, the clash of arms
> Incarnate love, exert thy charms
>   Lord Jesus quickly come!
>
> Hope of the sacramental host
> Their only joy, glory, and boast,
> Without [thy] advent all is lost!
>   Lord Jesus quickly come![14]

Even the once ebullient Benjamin Palmer spoke with increasing desperation as the war drew to a close. The diarist Mary Chesnut recorded

---

[13]Jack P. Maddex, Jr., "Proslavery Millennialism: Social Eschatology in Antebellum Calvinism," *American Quarterly* 31 (1979): 47-49, 60-61; Beringer, *Why the South Lost,* 495-96 n. 29; and Pamela Elwyn Thomas Colbenson, "Millennial Thought among Southern Evangelicals, 1830-1885" (Ph.D. diss., Georgia State University, 1980) 209-10, 215-17, 221-22.

[14]Colbenson, "Millennial Thought," 209-10.

the profound change that had occurred in Palmer's preaching since the
first exciting days of South Carolina's secession. "Went with Mrs. Rhett
to hear Dr. Palmer," Chesnut wrote. "I did not know before," she said,

> how utterly hopeless was our situation. This man is so eloquent. It was
> hard to listen and not give way. Despair was his word—and martyrdom.
> He offered us nothing more in this world than the martyr's crown. . . .
> Every day shows that slavery is doomed the world over. For that he thanked
> God. He spoke of these times of our agony. And then came the cry: "Help
> us, oh God. Vain is the help of man."

"And so we came away," Chesnut concluded, "shaken to the depths."[15]

As it turned out, the war had a crippling institutional effect on the
churches, and many years passed before church bodies in the South re-
gained either the financial stability or membership numbers that they had
enjoyed in the time before the war. The Methodists, for instance, who
suffered the most, saw a thirty percent decrease in membership from 1860
to 1866 and a loss of about fifty percent in some areas of charitable giving.
Almost the entire male population of the South was forced into military
service, the economy was devastated, regular ecclesiastical meetings were
disrupted or cancelled altogether, and church buildings were closed by
Union commanders. White Southerners lamented that the misfortunes of
war had caused many erstwhile Christians to neglect spiritual matters. They
agreed that the war had generally had a debilitating influence on religion
throughout their region. As historian W. Harrison Daniel has written, "the
popular notion that people turn to the church in time of war" was simply
not true in the civilian population of the South during the Civil War. Despite the religious enthusiasm that did develop in the Confederate army
during this period, most of the churches experienced mainly demoralization and a waning interest at home in the mid-1860s.[16]

A poignant letter from James Otey, bishop of the Episcopal diocese of
Tennessee, exemplifies the sorrow that many clergymen felt about the state
of their churches. Otey explained to his friend that he faced an extraordinarily difficult time during the war, for religious devotion was entirely lacking

---

[15]Mary Chesnut, *Mary Chesnut's Civil War*, ed. C. Vann Woodward (New Haven: Yale
University Press, 1981) 644.

[16]W. Harrison Daniel, "The Effects of the Civil War on Southern Protestantism,"
Maryland Historical Magazine 69 (1974): 58-59; and Hunter Dickinson Farish, *The Circuit-
Rider Dismounts: A Social History of Southern Methodism, 1865-1900* (New York: Da Capo
Press, 1969) 30-33.

among civilians in the South. "Our Ch[urch] matters seem to partake of the
nature of the Country, in the apathy indifference & positive neglect of duty"
of former churchgoers, Otey wrote. "At a time," he continued,

> when believers ought to be specially attentive to every duty & should feel
> stirred up to be earnest & fervent in prayers & supplications—they seem
> to be lukewarm or cold & even insensible.

The state of the churches was of great concern to religious leaders like Otey,
but there was little they thought could be done about it.[17]

In reaction to the often chaotic affairs of civilian parishes, the clergy
looked to the Confederate army camp as a more promising field for their
labors. As one clergyman wrote to a friend in 1864, "the heart of the people . . . is sound,—and that is in the army." Despite the number of "mam-
mon worshippers and skulkers" who congregated at home, he believed that
the churches might still have an impact on Southern men, if missionaries
were to go among the soldiers. In addition, the 1863 meeting of the Presbyterian synod of Virginia noted that there were "few things more extraordinary than the work of God in the army." What so amazed that group of
churchmen was the fact that in the army there was "more zeal, apparently,
for God and the salvation of souls, than . . . in the church at home."[18]

In light of this general pessimism concerning the war's effect on the
Southern churches, the work of the denominations in the Confederate
Army stands in especially sharp contrast. By the end of the war, saving
the souls of the men in the camps became the one hope that churchmen
could honestly uphold. And with the political collapse of their region,
Southern evangelicals had little choice but to emphasize the soldiers' on-
going need for a strong personal faith to see themselves through the crisis.
Leaders in the churches reminded individuals that they should seek religious meaning apart from the declining culture, and so the denominations
worked feverishly to save the souls of men in the Confederate armed forces.
Not expecting that the army mission would have much practical impact
on the outcome of the war, clergy prayed that it would at least bring the
joys of heaven to men who fell in battle. They also hoped that soldiers

---

[17]James Otey to William C. Gray, 10 January 1863, in the James H. Otey Papers, Jessie
Ball DuPont Library, University of the South, Sewanee TN.

[18]Wight, "Churches in the Confederacy," 69-76, 97-100; Ralph E. Luker, *A Southern
Tradition in Theology and Social Criticism, 1830-1930: The Religious Liberalism and Social
Conservatism of James Warley Miles, William Porcher DuBose and Edgar Gardner Murphy* (New
York: The Edwin Mellen Press, 1984) 146; Synod of Virginia (Presbyterian), *Minutes*
(1863): 339-40; and Presbyterian Church in the Confederate States of America, *Minutes
of the General Assembly* (1864): 278-79, 283-84.

who had been converted in the army would return home and become the firm foundation upon which the churches would be rebuilt after the war.

Arguments made by representatives of the Southern Baptist Convention are fairly typical of the attitudes of all the denominations. In 1863 the Baptists confirmed that the army was a fertile ground for missionary work. They recommended that ministers be released from their parishes for a short time each year to minister to the military forces. As the committee on army missions of the Convention made clear, the chance to preach to so many men at one time was unique: the soldiers were crowded together with time on their hands, and they were oppressed by the constant threat of death. "The time is short," the committee wrote, because soldiers, "the safeguard, the pride, the glory of the Confederacy," every day were "passing from the fields illustrated by their valor into a land of darkness and the shadow of death."[19]

Army life was said to foster an intensity of religious feeling that was virtually unknown in the civilian world. Baptists, for example, compared the solemn observance of the Sabbath by Confederate troops to a "Puritanic village," and Presbyterians linked revivals in Lee's army to the "unprecendented earnestness" with which soldiers received the preaching of the gospel. Many soldiers were said to have heard more religious instruction in camp than they had ever enjoyed before, and consequently they responded to preaching with unusual fervor. A Methodist tract expressed both the joy and the surprise that Southern Christians were feeling in a poem about the Lord's presence in seemingly God-forsaken places. "Pray in the camp! yes, in the camp / God hears and answers prayer," the poem remarked. "Our God is not confined to place," it continued,

> Not to the Temple's dome
> Doth He restrict His grace,
> But bids His kingdom come,
> Wherever there's a praying heart.
> In camp, as cloister-cell,
> To the praying heart He'll grace impart;
> What to Him, where we dwell?
> So that in view we keep the Cross—
> The Cross of Calvary;
> Thank God that everywhere on earth
> Our eyes that Cross can see.[20]

---

[19]Southern Baptist Convention, *Proceedings of the Ninth Biennial Sessions* (1863): 12, 16, 37, 52-54.

[20]Ibid., (1863): 37-38; Presbyterian Church in the Confederate States, *Minutes* (1864):

Fearing that soldiers, if left to themselves, would fall into hedonistic and licentious habits, Southern clergy resolved that their men would be supported at every turn by the restraining influences of religion. In an army considered by many to be woefully lacking in discipline, the Confederate soldier's expectation that he could behave in any manner he chose demanded curbing. As a religious tract distributed in the army illustrates, churchmen argued that the character of a good soldier could also be the character of a good Christian. A Christian soldier, unlike his unbelieving and careless comrades, would be disciplined, brave, persevering, and in all ways manly, for religious courage elevated men above the fear of mere physical death. Clergy also commended the piety that prevailed among some high-ranking officers like Stonewall Jackson and Robert E. Lee. Since many Southern generals were concerned about giving religious instruction to soldiers, churchmen felt reassured that their armies contained men who were zealously concerned with keeping God's commandments and converting sinners.[21]

The first practical steps to minister to the soldiers were undertaken by the Board of Domestic Missions of the Southern Baptist Convention. Early in 1862, the corresponding secretary of the Mission Board asked the missionary secretaries in the different states both to solicit money from congregations and urge the occasional release of ministers from their parish duties for service in the army. Certain clergy were also designated to act as supervisors of the work, meet with chaplains, and secure appointments for missionaries in the various field armies. By the end of the war, the Baptist Mission Board had employed seventy-eight missionaries, supplemented the salaries of eleven chaplains, and encouraged the short-term involvement of numerous other clergymen in the Confederate armed forces.[22]

318-19; and The Camp and the Cross (Richmond: Soldiers' Tract Association, M. E. Church, South, [186-]) 1-2, 7.

[21]W. H. Christian, The Importance of a Soldier Becoming a Christian (Richmond: Soldiers' Tract Association, M. E. Church, South, [186-]) 1-6; John D. Paris, A Sermon Preached Before Brig.-Gen. Hoke's Brigade, at Kinston, N. C., on the 28th of February, 1864 (Greensboro NC: A. W. Ingold & Co., 1864) 11-12; The Religious Herald 34 (1861): 75; Wight, "Churches in the Confederacy," 128-30; and David Donald, "Died of Democracy," in Why the North Won the Civil War, ed. David Donald (New York: Collier Books, 1973) 80-84.

[22]W. Harrison Daniel, "Southern Protestantism and Army Missions in the Confederacy," Mississippi Quarterly 17 (1964): 179-81; W. Harrison Daniel, "The Southern Baptists in the Confederacy," Civil War History 6 (1960): 396-97; and Southern Baptist Convention, Proceedings (1863): 53-54.

The next denomination to involve itself with the army was the Presbyterian Church, which at its 1863 General Assembly resolved to direct its missionary attention during the war to the soldiers. Within the next year, the Committee on Domestic Missions gave a large portion of its funds to sixty ministers who were working in the army. The General Assembly, too, appointed special commissioners for each of the major armies of the Confederacy. These men not only functioned as chaplains themselves, but also recruited chaplains for regiments that lacked them and acted as intermediaries between Presbyterians in the army and the central denomination. From mid-1863 to mid-1865, the church spent more than $100,000 to support the 130 Presbyterian clergymen who ministered to the troops at the height of their denomination's involvement.[23]

The decisions of the Baptists and Presbyterians to make these institutional commitments to the army were motivated in part by their awareness that the Confederate chaplaincy just was not adequate to minister effectively to the men in the camps. Although each regiment should have had an active chaplain assigned to it, less that half the units ever had the services of a chaplain. The Presbyterians in particular complained that the War Department did not pay chaplains a large enough salary or provide them with sufficient status to entice capable clergymen to serve in the army. As Moses Drury Hoge wrote to the chairman of the government's Committee of Military Affairs, "men of the experience learning & piety" who would otherwise want to devote themselves to the chaplain's work could not afford to do so under the system then established. Churchmen feared, therefore, that the religious situation in the Confederate army was confused and chaotic. The government refused to take control, and left the initiative almost exclusively in the hands of the individual units and the denominations to bring soldiers the spiritual ministrations that they otherwise would have lacked.[24]

The Methodist Episcopal Church, South, proved to be the most active denomination in sending ministers into the Confederate army as

---

[23]Daniel, "Southern Protestantism and Army Missions," 181-82; Sidney J. Romero, *Religion in the Rebel Ranks* (Lanham MD: University Press of America, 1983) 16; Presbyterian Church in the Confederate States, *Minutes* (1863): 138-40; ibid., (1864): 278-79, 314-22; and Beverly Tucker Lacy to his cousin from New Market VA, 14 December 1864, in the Beverly Tucker Lacy Papers, Southern Historical Collection, Library of the University of North Carolina at Chapel Hill.

[24]Moses Drury Hoge to W. P. Miles from Richmond, 7 March 1862, in the Moses Drury Hoge Papers, Virginia Historical Society, Richmond; and Presbyterian Church in the Confederate States, *Minutes* (1863): 161.

chaplains. Consequently, it was not until the General Conference in the spring of 1863 that the church decided to adopt a special plan of its own for army missions. At that time, bishops were requested to appoint specially designated missionaries to the several military departments; those men (like the Baptist army supervisors and the Presbyterian army commissioners) were to travel throughout their departments, preach and minister pastorally to the soldiers, and report back to their bishops about their work. By the beginning of 1864 the Methodist conferences were supporting thirty-five full-time missionaries and augmenting the salaries of twenty-one army chaplains.[25]

The efforts of the other church bodies were far less organized than those of the three largest denominations, but even they had an impact on the religious life of the Confederate armies. Although the Episcopal Church did not fund an army mission as such, the bishop of each diocese undertook his own personal ministry in the army. They visited the camps on numerous occasions, preached to and counseled the soldiers, and baptized and confirmed converts. The Lutheran Church for its part formed an executive committee on army missions to coordinate the work of its ministers; in addition, the Lutheran synods of Tennessee, Virginia, South Carolina, and North Carolina appointed special missionaries to serve in the armies. As a result of the missionary work these smaller denominations performed, most prominent clergymen in the South were at one time or another involved in the ministry to the Confederate troops.[26]

Southern churchmen also employed religious tracts and newspapers, Bibles, and hymn and prayer books as ways to reach the men in uniform. Despite a chronic lack of funds and a shortage of paper—problems from which the publishers of these materials suffered throughout the war—Christians nevertheless did the best they could to maintain their printing operations. And according to many reports, this reading matter enjoyed a large and enthusiastic audience in the Southern camps. As the *Richmond Christian Advocate* remarked, tracts were usually "the most effectual means of saving our army from the demoralizing influences of camp life." From his visits to the field, Presbyterian minister William James Hoge knew that the soldiers were always eager for something to read, but too frequently they were not discriminating about the quality of what they found. Hoge hoped that the churches would supply suitable literature, especially "Tes-

---

[25]Daniel, "Southern Protestantism and Army Missions," 182-83; *Army and Navy Messenger for the Trans-Mississippi Department* (2 March 1865) [no pagination]; and *Richmond Christian Advocate* 20 (30 July 1863): 2.

[26]Daniel, "Southern Protestantism and Army Missions," 183.

taments," because with those in their hands, he thought, many Southern soldiers could surely be converted.[27]

Coinciding with the lead they took in sending missionaries to the soldiers, the Southern Baptists also enjoyed a formidable advantage over the other denominations in the publication of religious literature for the army. Since the Baptists' Sunday School and Colportage Board had been distributing pamphlets for many years before the war, an organization already existed that could send representatives of the denomination with reading material into the camps. The wartime demand for devotional materials was also responsible for the creation of new agencies that produced religious literature for the troops. Among these organizations was the interdenominational Evangelical Tract Society of Petersburg, Virginia, which was the largest and most prolific of these organizations. The year 1863 alone saw the founding of five religious newspapers designed for circulation among members of the Confederate armed forces: the *Army and Navy Herald* and the *Soldier's Paper* (Soldiers' Tract Association, Methodist Episcopal Church, South); the *Army and Navy Messenger* (Evangelical Tract Society); the *Soldier's Friend* (Baptists in Atlanta); and the *Soldier's Visitor* (Committee of Publication, Presbyterian Church in the Confederate States).[28]

Unlike their counterparts in the North, who felt the war was a wholesome calamity that invigorated both religion and culture in their region, Southern Christians were hard pressed to find positive effects of the war upon life at home. They were heartened, however, by the results of evangelization among the Confederate troops. Maintaining the separation of church and state not only by design but also by necessity, Southern churchmen undertook a vigorous army mission that was wholly independent of their government. The success they achieved with the soldiers further confirmed their long-standing prejudice against the church's cooperation with the state. With little aid or encouragement from Confederate officials, the denominations' leaders believed that they had main-

---

[27]*Richmond Christian Advocate* 20 (1 May 1862): 2; ibid. (9 April 1863): 2; William James Hoge to Robert Lewis Dabney from Charlottesville VA, 13 December 1862, in the Hoge Family Papers, Historical Foundation of the Presbyterian and Reformed Churches, Montreat NC; and Myers, *Children of Pride*, 1097.

[28]Romero, *Religion in the Rebel Ranks*, 91-98, 102-104, 147-64; and Henry Smith Stroupe, *The Religious Press in the South Atlantic States, 1802-1865* (Durham NC: Duke University Press, 1956) 34-35, 42-43, 102-103.

tained a strong religious interest within the army camps. And when the Confederacy was destroyed and the South lay physically devastated after the war, churchmen could point with pride to what *they* had accomplished with the army. Southern soldiers had gained there a spiritual prize of far more enduring value, the clergy thought, than the mere carnal excitement of a worldly victory.

Holy Joes: The Experience of Clergy in the Armies

3

In his perceptive memoirs of his service in the Union army, Newton Martin Curtis, formerly colonel of the 16th New York Regiment, described the activities of a chaplain whom he knew. Curtis wrote about this minister with words of the highest possible praise and said that he combined "fortitude, courage, devotion, and a just sense of duty" in a way that attained "the superlative of the sublime in human action." During the battle of Salem Heights in May 1863, "Chaplain Hall" had advanced unarmed with his regiment in the attack on the Confederate position. He kept in step with his men, and when they fell, he administered aid to those he could help and assisted the stretcher-bearers in carrying off the more seriously wounded. Curtis thought that Hall had "possessed a most splendid courage and a devotion to duty that took no account of danger," and he recorded with pride that the War Department awarded Hall the Congressional Medal of Honor for his heroism in " 'voluntarily exposing himself to heavy fire during the thickest of the fight.' " Curtis was proud that this chaplain exemplified the ideals on which the United States army chaplaincy was based.[1]

Prior to 1861, however, the military chaplaincy had been so small that clergy in the army had few chances to make much of an impact on the lives of American soldiers. A law enacted in March 1859, for example, allowed the appointment of only 30 chaplains for the 19 regiments and

---

[1]Newton Martin Curtis, *From Bull Run to Chancellorsville: The Story of the Sixteenth New York Infantry Together with Personal Reminiscences* (New York: G. P. Putnam's Sons, 1906) 266-67.

198 companies composing the regular army during peacetime. But the coming of the Civil War produced a tremendous change, since 30 clergymen were clearly unable to minister to the 650 regiments of infantry and cavalry that entered Federal service in the spring and summer of 1861. President Lincoln especially was concerned that an effective chaplaincy should be formed to give spiritual support to the Northern soldiers. General Orders Nos. 15 and 16 (of 4 May 1861), therefore, stipulated that colonels of both the regular and volunteer regiments must appoint a chaplain for their units, and that the minister so chosen had to be elected by the vote of the officers of the regiment. The chaplain was expected to be an ordained minister of a Christian denomination and was to receive a salary corresponding to that of a captain of cavalry, a sum equal to about $1,700 a year.[2]

Lincoln and the War Department recognized the value of religion as a unifying force in the army; therefore, they instructed chaplains to maintain "the social happiness and moral improvement of the troops" and report regularly on the "moral and religious condition" of their regiments. Army regulations also directed chaplains to hold worship services whenever possible and ordered that the regimental officers were to assist the clergy in fulfilling this obligation. Since church and state in the United States were officially separated, these orders had to be left somewhat vague, and thus the exact frequency of the services and their form were left to the discretion of the individual chaplain and his commander.[3]

As a result of the unprecedented growth in the size of both the army and the chaplaincy, problems with the system soon developed. On reviewing the salary of the chaplains, for instance, some members of Congress worried that those men were being overpaid. In the spring and summer of 1862, the Senate debated a bill that would have limited the number of chaplains to only one man per brigade and, thereby, would have reduced the amount of money needed to pay clergymen in the army. Although Congress rejected the bill and allowed the assignment of one chaplain per

---

[2]Lorenzo D. Johnson, *Chaplains of the General Government, With Objections to Their Employment Considered* (New York: Sheldon, Blakeman & Co., 1856) 70; Herman Albert Norton, *Struggling for Recognition: The United States Army Chaplaincy, 1791-1865*, vol. 2 of *History of the United States Army Chaplaincy* (Washington DC: Office of the Chief of Chaplains, Department of the Army, 1977) 83; and United States War Department, *The War of the Rebellion: A Compilation of the Official Records of the Union and Confederate Armies* (Washington DC: Government Printing Office, 1880-1901) series 3, 1:154, 157.

[3]Ibid., series 3, 1:382; ibid., series 3, 4:227-28; [Robert W. Landis], "Chaplaincy in the Army," *The Danville Quarterly Review* 3 (1863): 256.

regiment to remain in force for the duration of the war, it did cut the chaplains' salaries to $1,200 a year. The lawmakers expected that this measure would not only save the government money in its payments to those chaplains who continued to serve faithfully in the army, but also force clergymen who entered military service for financial, not patriotic, reasons to resign. The new, reduced salary stayed in effect until the war ended three years later.[4]

One of the most troubling problems regarding the status of chaplains concerned their pay. The 1862 law that reduced the chaplains' pay stipulated (innocently enough) that they should receive a monthly salary of "one hundred dollars and two rations a day when on duty." Although Congress intended the phrase "when on duty" to modify only "two rations a day," some literalistic paymasters decided that all compensation should be witheld from chaplains who were not present for duty, whether absent on leave, sick, wounded, or captured by the enemy. Payment procedures for chaplains who were on duty were awkward, too. In order for a chaplain to receive his pay, his colonel had to testify that he had done his work and was owed his money; the word of the chaplain himself was not sufficient. Because no other officer was treated in this manner, chaplains complained about what one minister called this "outrageous decision" that selected clergy "for special insult."[5]

Questions related to professional standards for chaplains demanded attention as well, for some colonels were said to have appointed men who were neither physically nor morally fit to serve. During the first rush of men to join the army, chaplaincies occasionally were obtained by those more renowned for their congeniality with officers than for their pastoral or spiritual commitment. Chaplains also tended to be young and inexperienced clergymen seeking opportunities that were denied them at home. As William Locke, the chaplain of the 11th Pennsylvania Regiment, remembered the situation, the early days of the war commonly saw "some valiant captain, anxious to have his favorite doctor or parson transformed into a surgeon or chaplain." Many incompetent men held positions of authority at that time, but later "the right men gravitated into the right places." Similar to other untested officers who streamed into the Union

---

[4]Roy J. Honeywell, *Chaplains of the United States Army* (Washington DC: Office of the Chief of Chaplains, Department of the Army, 1958) 104; and Norton, *Struggling for Recognition*, 89.

[5]Alonzo H. Quint, *The Potomac and the Rapidan: Army Notes* (Boston: Crosby and Nichols, 1864) 353-54; *Official Records*, series 3, 1:368, 375; and ibid., series 3, 4:227-28.

army in 1861, chaplains likewise were forced to learn their skills through hard trials in camp and battle.[6]

In response to these troubles, Congress ruled in July 1862 that only a man who was "a regularly ordained minister of some religious denomination" and could present testimonials of good standing in his denomination would be allowed to become a chaplain. Congress thereby attempted to provide measures that would bring men with proper ecclesiastical credentials into the chaplaincy, give the denominations some control over the process by which chaplains were chosen, and encourage the dismissal of unsuitable chaplains from the service. Orders from the War Department in the summer and fall of 1862, furthermore, specifically instructed regimental commanders to evaluate the fitness and efficiency of chaplains already in the army and discharge those who had not done what was expected of them.[7]

Additionally, there was implicit in this act the provision for non-Christian chaplains. Since the original law of 1861 stated that chaplains had to be Christians, Jews had been officially barred as army chaplains. Although the government intended to be neutral regarding religion, most lawmakers assumed that chaplains would almost certainly be Protestant Christians and had said as much in the first law they passed. However important the revision was as a symbolic gesture, the change really had little practical effect. In 1861, one unordained Jew had served briefly as the chaplain of the 5th Pennsylvania Cavalry, but he had had to resign when the illegality of his appointment was exposed by a Y. M. C. A. worker visiting the regiment. And only one rabbi (Ferdinand Sarner of the 54th New York) is known to have served as a regimental chaplain after such an appointment became legal.[8]

The situation for Roman Catholics—another minority religious group in the midst of a predominantly Protestant army—was perhaps even more frustrating than that faced by Jews. Two priests had accompanied the

---

[6]Philip Eugene Howard, *The Life Story of Henry Clay Trumbull: Army Chaplain, Editor, and Author* (Philadelphia: The Sunday School Times Co., 1905) 184-85; William Henry Locke, *The Story of the Regiment* (New York: James Miller, 1872) 38-39; [Landis], "Chaplaincy in the Army," 258-59; Quint, *Potomac and the Rapidan*, 290; and Bell Irvin Wiley, " 'Holy Joes' of the Sixties: A Study of Civil War Chaplains," *Huntington Library Quarterly* 16 (1953): 290-92.

[7]*Official Records*, series 3, 1:728; ibid., series 3, 2:278, 398, 519, 651; and Norton, *Struggling for Recognition*, 85-90.

[8]Bertram Wallace Korn, *American Jewry and the Civil War* (Philadelphia: Jewish Publication Society of America, 1951) 84, 88.

American army under special presidential appointment during the Mexican War, and three others had been employed as post chaplains in the 1850s, but Roman Catholic clergy were not allowed to serve in sizable numbers until the Civil War. Even then, their numbers were small in comparison to the Protestant chaplains in the army. This relative shortage, though, resulted not from a lack of Catholic soldiers to whom priests could minister, but from the refusal of Protestant officers to accept priests as chaplains for their Catholic men. In the spring of 1862, for instance, when the proportion of Roman Catholic to Protestant soldiers was approximately 1 to 6, only 22 priests served among the 472 Union chaplains then on duty. Catholic chaplains were chosen only in regiments that were entirely Catholic; in regiments that were partially Catholic, the chaplain was almost invariably Protestant.[9]

Clergymen of all denominations believed that army regulations were not sufficiently specific about the status of chaplains. In the matter of the chaplains' proper dress, General Order No. 102 of 1861 stipulated that the uniform was to be a "plain black frock coat, with standing collar, and one row of nine black buttons; plain black pantaloons; black felt hat, or army forage cap, without ornament." Chaplains often appeared more like civilian clergymen, then, than like standard military figures. This also presented a special problem for one black chaplain. Henry M. Turner complained to the Secretary of War that the lack of distinguishing marks on his uniform often resulted in the indignity of his being mistaken for a private by white soldiers. He asked that chaplains be allowed to wear "some special mark, either a strap on the soldier, or a stripe on the arm," so that they would not be hindered from performing their necessary duties.[10]

Chaplains were not officially treated as officers until April 1864, when Congress ruled that chaplains deserved the respect accorded to commissioned officers, and were to hold "the rank of chaplain, without command" and be listed with surgeons on the rolls of the field staff of the regiment. Yet even after that congressional action was passed, many com-

---

[9]Norton, *Struggling for Recognition*, 93; and Benjamin J. Blied, *Catholics and the Civil War* (Milwaukee: N.p., 1945) 112-13.

[10]George H. Williams, "The Chaplaincy in the Armed Forces of the United States of America in Historical and Ecclesiastical Perspective," in *Military Chaplains: From a Religious Military to a Military Religion*, ed. Harvey Cox (New York: American Report Press, 1971) 37; Honeywell, *Chaplains*, 110; Ira Berlin, ed., *The Black Military Experience*, Freedom, A Documentary History of Emancipation, series 2 (Cambridge: Cambridge University Press, 1982) 359; and [Robert W. Landis], "The Army Chaplain's Manual, by J. Pinkney Hammond," *The Danville Quarterly Review* 3 (1863): 571-81.

manders still considered the term "chaplain" to connote a title rather than a grade. Although the Adjutant General proposed that the law should be amended so that the chaplain's rank would correspond exactly to that of captain, the war ended before Congress could further clarify this confused issue.[11]

As a result of their often uncertain military position, some Union chaplains thought they should function as combatants. The draft laws of 1863 and 1864, after all, had not excluded ministers from its provisions, and clergymen who were drafted to be soldiers were expected to fight for their country. The status of chaplains as different from ordinary clergy in

A group of Union IX Corps chaplains pose before their tent near Petersburg, Virginia (photograph courtesy of the Library of Congress).

---

[11]Honeywell, *Chaplains*, 110; and *Official Records*, series 3, 4:227-28, 809.

the army, however, was made clear when the War Department decided in the spring of 1863 that chaplains were noncombatants. The United States government declared that it would not hold Confederate chaplains as prisoners of war and ordered that they were to be released immediately if ever captured in a battle. Chaplains were presumed, therefore, to be assisting the war effort with spiritual resources alone.[12]

Despite these military statutes, a few chaplains still worried about what they considered to be their passive role. For some of these men, the solution was to serve as staff officers, working at headquarters while remaining technically outside of combat. For others, the act of accompanying soldiers to the front, rallying or commanding them when the occasion demanded, but at the same time bearing no weapons, seemed to be the best answer. Henry Clay Trumbull, chaplain of the 10th Connecticut Regiment, said that the primary function of the chaplain ought to be as a morale officer; a chaplain, he believed, was worth at least one hundred men in battle. Indeed, in an era when morale and firepower were equally important during battle, a clergyman's bravery may well have been a valuable resource to his regiment.[13]

Since Federal law required that a chaplain be chosen after a regiment had organized itself, a clergyman needed to make himself known to the officers of the unit while it was forming. Although most clergy first entered camp as visitors whom the colonel had invited to meet the men, some ministers actually enlisted in the regiment and then sought election to the chaplaincy as a man coming from the ranks of the soldiers. Officers were said to have prized such action and considered it to be the most effective way for chaplains to win the respect of their men.[14]

---

[12]Rollin W. Quimby, "The Chaplains' Predicament," *Civil War History* 8 (1962): 25; Honeywell, *Chaplains*, 105-106; James F. Childress, *Moral Responsibilities in Conflicts: Essays on Nonviolence, War, and Conscience* (Baton Rouge: Louisiana State University Press, 1982) 143; *Official Records*, series 3, 3:154; and ibid., series 3, 4:27-28, 288, 795.

[13]Henry Clay Trumbull, *War Memories of an Army Chaplain* (Philadelphia: Charles Scribner's Sons, 1898) 5; Howard, *Life Story of Henry Clay Trumbull*, 220-21, 231-32; Clay MacCauley, *Memories and Memorials: Gatherings from an Eventful Life* (Tokyo: The Fukuin Printing Co., Ltd., 1914) 638; Rollin W. Quimby, "Recurrent Themes and Purposes in the Sermons of Union Army Chaplains," *Speech Monographs* 31 (1964): 425-36; and Wiley, " 'Holy Joes,' " 298-99.

[14]Robert McAllister, *The Civil War Letters of General Robert McAllister*, ed. James I. Robertson, Jr. (New Brunswick NJ: Rutgers University Press, 1965) 570, 584; and Richard Eddy, *History of the Sixtieth New York State Volunteers* (Philadelphia: The author, 1864) 6-12.

Numerous stories are to be found in the literature of the Civil War about the more militant clergy who laid aside their clerical gowns, took up rifles and swords, and entered the struggle like other men. Although not all these stories are factual, many certainly do have the ring of truth. Arthur Fuller, for example, served as a sharpshooter in the attack on Fredericksburg in 1862 and was killed in the battle. In spite of the expiration of his term as chaplain of the 16th Massachusetts Regiment, Fuller volunteered for the hazardous duty of driving the Confederates out of the city. Approval of such reckless behavior was certainly not universal in the Union army, but a fair number of Northern soldiers *were* impressed by clergymen who demonstrated bravery under fire. As the officers of the 106th New York wrote to the minister they called to be their chaplain, a rifle used by a clergyman in battle might potentially be "an instrument in God's hands to work out divine ends."[15]

Clergy who enlisted as chaplains were, of course, swayed by a variety of motives, both conscious and unconscious. They were certainly no different from their other countrymen who also served in the military during the crisis of the Union. Most believed that love of country and concern for the souls of those whose lives were threatened impelled them to become chaplains. Equating the cause of their nation with the cause of God, they entered the army with clear consciences; rather than deserting the ministry and their parishes at home, they discovered a higher calling and a greater usefulness in the camp. At a moment when all citizens were united in a common struggle, the duties of a minister and of a patriot seemed to be thoroughly compatible, perhaps almost identical. Chaplains thought that they were in a unique position to inspire men to fight, protect them from the vices of camp, and bring their souls spotless to Christ in the world to come.[16]

---

[15]Richard Frederick Fuller, *Chaplain Fuller: Being a Life Sketch of a New England Clergyman and Army Chaplain* (Boston: Walker, Wise and Co., 1863) 299-302; and letter from the officers of the 106th New York Regiment to Richard Eddy, North Mountain VA, 4 April 1863, in the Richard Eddy Papers, Andover-Harvard Theological Library, Harvard Divinity School, Cambridge MA.

[16]John R. Adams, *Memorial and Letters of Rev. John R. Adams, D.D.* (Cambridge MA: Privately printed, 1890) 18; William Y. Brown, *The Army Chaplain: His Office, Duties, and Responsibilities, and the Means of Aiding Him* (Philadelphia: W. S. & A. Martien, 1863) 126-27; Trumbull, *War Memories*, 3-4; Amos S. Billingsley, *From the Flag to the Cross: or, Scenes and Incidents of Christianity in the War* (Philadelphia: New-World Publishing Company, 1872) 413-16; and James B. Rogers, *War Pictures: Experiences and Observations of a Chaplain in the U.S. Army in the War of the Southern Rebellion* (Chicago: Church & Goodman, 1863) 14.

The reflections of a Unitarian chaplain about the experience of defeat at First Bull Run reveal how Northern chaplains wove together the themes of patriotism and religious duty. This man published his thoughts in an article in *The Monthly Journal* of his denomination, in which he argued that the true purpose of the war would be realized in the "discipline" and "purification" of the American people. Although life in the army camp could eventually lead to demoralized behavior by troops uninstructed by chaplains and pious officers, a man's first experiences as a soldier unquestionably produced "an incitement of religious feeling." Following the call of duty from one's country reminded men of their religious calling as well, and facing danger in battle encouraged them to place their reliance on God throughout that experience. Just as a fresh breeze clears the air on a hot summer's day, this chaplain wrote, "so this fresh gale of duty and patriotism set in upon our worldly life, and . . . made it clear and generous and pure." The war was going to demonstrate how the bravest and strongest regiments were usually formed by soldiers who were the most religious. Because of the involvement of religious men in the national cause, therefore, Northerners could trust that the rebellion would be crushed and the Union would prevail.[17]

Black chaplains even more than whites spoke with confidence about the involvement of God in their nation's struggle against the defenders of slavery. William H. Hunter was a chaplain of one of the black regiments that helped liberate Wilmington, North Carolina. On the Sunday after that city fell to Union forces, he spoke from a church pulpit about the Northern victory. The military triumph gave Hunter the greatest personal satisfaction, because he was returning to a region where he had formerly been a slave. He told the congregation that he had once been enslaved, but now was free, and all the blacks in the South would soon be free as well. Hunter addressed the black men and women who sat before him that day and asked them to remember that their release from captivity and entrance into freedom was a divine gift. To a "tumultuous uproar" from the ex-slaves, he exclaimed, "Thank God the armies of the Lord and of Gideon has [sic] triumphed and the Rebels have been driven back in confusion and scattered like chaff before the wind."[18]

The adaptation Northern chaplains made to the daily realities of army life was nowhere more apparent than in the themes they employed in their

---

[17]*The Monthly Journal of the American Unitarian Association* 2 (1861): 497-99, 502-503, 508.

[18]Leon F. Litwack, *Been in the Storm So Long: The Aftermath of Slavery* (New York: Alfred A. Knopf, 1979) 465-66.

sermons. Two subjects were predominant: the patriotic requirement to fight for one's country and the personal need for each man to make spiritual preparations for death when fulfilling his patriotic duties. Most chaplains assumed that country and God had absolute and parallel claims to a man's soul and to his body. The nation might rightly expect men to surrender their lives for its cause; the hope that religion offered was the prospect that such sacrifices would be fruitful ones and in accordance with God's will. The pious soldier who died in the service of his country had nothing to fear in death, for if his soul were prepared, he would immediately receive his reward in God's kingdom. As a chaplain advised his men in a sermon, those who gave themselves sacrificially in the "baptism of blood" of the war would be truly blessed by God.[19]

The obligation to hold worship services—the one duty actually specified for the chaplain—was sometimes hard to discharge. Whether a chaplain's unit was currently bivouacked in camp or active in the field, difficulties frequently prevented him from leading worship. If the army were stationary for a time, poor weather, Sunday morning drills, or the entrance of new recruits into camp could interfere with services. If the regiment were on the march or about to engage in battle, on the other hand, chaplains seldom even attempted to hold formal worship. Circumstances compelled them, therefore, to devise informal methods of corporate prayer. They often led their men in spontaneous worship whenever the routine of military life allowed them such an opportunity. Some chaplains considered such impromptu worship to be preferable to all other forms. Services in the open air were said to be far more uplifting than those in civilian churches—"cushioned seats" and a "hot, confined, four-walled building" not being comparable to the glories of nature. Most clergy probably would have preferred that religious life in the army follow civilian routine, but they accepted the inevitability of many of the inconveniences of worship in the camps.[20]

---

[19]Quimby, "Recurrent Themes," 428-33; Henry Clay Trumbull, *Desirableness of Active Service: A Sermon Preached to the Tenth Connecticut Regiment* (Hartford: Case, Lockwood and Company, 1864) 10, 12-13, 16-18, 20; Henry Clay Trumbull, *Good News! A Sermon Preached to the Veteran Volunteers of the 10th Connecticut Regiment* (Hartford: Case, Lockwood and Company, 1864) 4, 16-18; and Henry Clay Trumbull, *A Good Record: A Sermon Preached . . . to the Tenth Connecticut Regiment* (Hartford: Case, Lockwood and Company, 1864) 6, 15.

[20]Quint, *Potomac and the Rapidan*, 11-13, 182; Charles A. Humphreys, *Field, Camp, Hospital, and Prison Cell in the Civil War, 1863-1865* (Boston: George H. Ellis Co., 1918) 12; John J. Hight, *History of the Fifty-Eighth Regiment of Indiana Volunteer Infantry*, comp.

Because there were few responsibilities that chaplains were required to perform, ministers sought out a variety of unofficial roles in the hopes of winning the support and acceptance of their men. As Frederic Denison, chaplain of the 1st Rhode Island Cavalry, complained, the chaplain was assigned "no appointed or recognized place," and in many cases he became "a supernumerary, a kind of fifth wheel to a coach." In this situation, any activity that provided either mercy or comfort to sufferers was looked upon as a worthy extension of a clergyman's ministry, and chap-

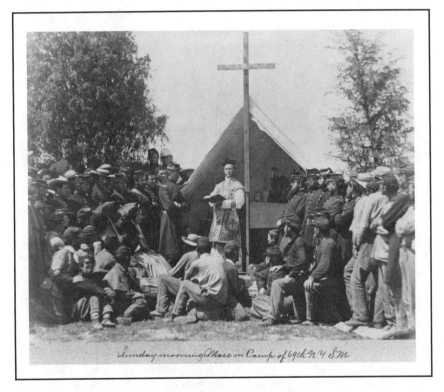

Sunday morning Mass in Camp of 69th N.Y. S.M.

Officers and men of the 69th New York Regiment attend Sunday mass. The Rev. Thomas H. Mooney is the celebrant (photograph courtesy of the Library of Congress).

Gilbert R. Stormont (Princeton IN: Press of the Clarion, 1895) 270, 292; James B. Rogers, *War Pictures: Experiences and Observations of a Chaplain in the U. S. Army in the War of the Southern Rebellion* (Chicago: Church & Goodman, 1863) 234-35; and Adams, *Memorial*, 18.

lains found in time that there were always small services of a practical nature that they could perform for their regiment. None of these activities
required skills learned in seminary, yet a chaplain undertook them since
he alone of all the soldiers in a regiment had the freedom to do them. As
Leonard Bacon noted in his *History of American Christianity*, Civil War
chaplains learned "a right apostolic sense to become all things to all men."[21]

The chaplain performed a variety of useful tasks in his regiment. He
wrote letters for hospitalized soldiers, acted as postmaster for his unit,
maintained a library stocked with religious and secular literature, taught
soldiers how to read and write, informed families of the deaths of loved
ones, aided the freed blacks who flocked to the armies, carried men and
equipment on horseback during marches, dug wells and rifle-pits in camp,
and foraged for fresh vegetables for his men. At the time of battle, the
chaplain was expected to assist wounded soldiers, and he was usually stationed in the rear of the regiment near the field hospital in a position where
he could help the surgeons. By aiding the wounded of both sides, chaplains believed that they provided an important contribution as Christians
in overcoming the horrors of war. Most were "good men, anxious to do
their duty" (as one clergyman concluded after the war), and they sought
opportunities in army life that would demonstrate their effectiveness both
as ministers and as patriots.[22]

In total, approximately 2,300 chaplains served in the Union armies
during the four years of the war, though no more than 600 were ever on
duty at one time. Of the major denominations, Methodists supplied close
to a third of all chaplains, followed in order by Presbyterians, Episcopa-

---

[21]Leonard Bacon, *A History of American Christianity*, vol. 13 of the American Church
History Series (New York: The Christian Literature Co., 1898) 349; and Frederic Deni-
son, "A Chaplain's Experience in the Union Army," in *Personal Narratives of Events in the
War of the Rebellion: Being Papers Read before the Rhode Island Soldiers and Sailors Historical
Society*, 4th ser. (Providence: The Society, 1893) 20:15-16.

[22]For examples of these various activities, see John William DeForest, *A Volunteer's
Adventures: A Union Captain's Record of the Civil War*, ed. James H. Croushore (New Haven: Yale University Press, 1946) 76; Denison, "Chaplain's Experience," 23; Rogers, *War
Pictures*, 85; Jonathan Pinkney Hammond, *The Army Chaplain's Manual, Designed as a Help
to Chaplains in the Discharge of Their Various Duties* (Philadelphia: J. P. Lippincott & Co.,
1863) 72-76, 83-85, 91-94, 99-100; Moses D. Gage, *From Vicksburg to Raleigh; or, a Complete History of the Twelfth Regiment Indiana Volunteer Infantry* (Chicago: Clarke & Co.,
1865) 51; John Eaton, *Grant, Lincoln, and the Freedmen: Reminiscences of the Civil War* (New
York: Longmans, Green, and Co., 1907) 27-28; Emory M. Stevens, "Story of the Chaplain," in *The Story of Our Regiment: A History of the 148th Pennsylvania Vols.*, ed. J. W.
Muffly (Des Moines IA: The Kenyon Printing & Mfg. Co., 1904) 196; and Berlin, *Black
Military Experience*, 620-25.

lians, Baptists, Congregationalists, Roman Catholics, and Unitarians. Although Baptists were at least equal to Methodists in the number of church members at this time, Baptist clergy by and large preferred to eschew the church-state involvement that the chaplaincy represented and sought service instead as volunteer missionaries for their denomination.[23]

The average length of time that chaplains stayed in the army was eighteen months, and very few remained with their original regiments for the entire war. The surplus of candidates for military chaplaincies that had existed in 1861 soon evaporated, and by the end of the second year of the war a shortage of chaplains began to make itself felt. By that time, chaplains had been killed, physically disabled by wounds and disease, recalled by their civilian churches, or had simply lost interest in the work in the army. Circumstances in the Iron Brigade, probably the most famous brigade in the Union army, were typical. In the five regiments that comprised that brigade, only the chaplain of the 24th Michigan stayed with his unit for its entire muster period. Although the second chaplain of the 7th Wisconsin served for nearly three years, the regiment's original chaplain left the army after only a brief period. The 19th Indiana had two unsuccessful chaplains, and the 6th Wisconsin had three, all of whom remained for only a short while. And the 2nd Wisconsin lost its chaplain early in 1862 and continued for the rest of the war without one.[24]

Unlike the United States government, which recognized the value of providing spiritual care for soldiers through its support of military chaplains, the Confederacy intentionally excluded the chaplaincy from the original organization of its army. There were several reasons for this exclusion. First, some Southern leaders (President Jefferson Davis and Secretary of War James Seddon, most notably) had a low opinion of the quality of their clergy; they thought that ministers would be more useful to the

[23]Norton, *Struggling for Recognition*, 108-109, 111n.; Quimby, "Chaplains' Predicament," 36; Wiley, " 'Holy Joes'," 290; William Warren Sweet, *Methodist Episcopal Church and the Civil War* (Cincinnati: Methodist Book Concern Press, 1912) 138-39; Lewis G. Vander Velde, *Presbyterian Churches and the Federal Union, 1861-1869* (Cambridge MA: Harvard University Press, 1932) 429; Aidan Henry Germain, *Catholic Military and Naval Chaplains, 1776-1917* (Washington DC: N.p., 1929) 55-134; and Samuel A. Eliot, ed., *Heralds of a Liberal Faith*, vol. 3, *The Preachers* (Boston: American Unitarian Association, 1910) 131-33.

[24]Wiley, " 'Holy Joes'," 290; Quimby, "Chaplains' Predicament," 29-30; and Alan T. Nolan, *The Iron Bridge: A Military History* (Madison: The State Historical Society of Wisconsin, 1975) 202-203.

country as soldiers than as preachers. Second, other Southerners were op-
posed to organizing a chaplaincy out of loyalty to ecclesiastical theories
concerning the strict separation of church and state; they believed that it
was the responsibility of the churches, not the government, to support
ministers in the army. Southern Baptists, for instance, consistently asked
for chaplains to be paid by their denominations rather than by the public
treasury. And third, the Confederacy itself had been founded on the principle of decentralized power, and many aspects of its political and military
life were either poorly organized or left intentionally to individual initiative. The situation regarding the chaplaincy, therefore, exemplified the
type of confusion that plagued the entire Confederate bureaucracy.[25]

The combination of these diverse factors meant that clergy in the
Confederate army would always feel out of place in their military role. Even
when a howl of protest from many church members forced the government to reconsider its initial action and establish a fledgling chaplaincy,
the damage to the esteem of the Southern clerical profession had already
been done. Unsure of what its position should be toward religion in the
army, the Confederate Congress directed President Davis to assign as many
chaplains as he deemed expedient to regiments, brigades, and military posts
and to set their pay at $85 a month, a figure that stood midway between
the salaries of a first and a second lieutenant. This legislation stipulated
(in its vague fashion) absolutely no regulations regarding age, physical
condition, or ecclesiastical standing, and it prescribed no duties, uniform,
or rank for the chaplains. Clergymen who enlisted as chaplains were going
to be left to themselves to decide how they could best serve their men and
the Confederate cause.[26]

Within two weeks following this legislation, however, the Congress
again undercut the clergy and amended its act so that the chaplains' sti-
pends would be reduced from $85 to $50 a month. Some legislators said
that they supported this reduction as part of their continuing opposition
to ministers' being paid by the government at all, while others claimed
that low salaries would prevent clergymen who were interested only in
material gain from entering the chaplaincy. The comment of a Mississippi

---

[25]Herman Albert Norton, "The Organization and Function of the Confederate Mili-
tary Chaplaincy, 1861-1865" (Ph.D. diss., Vanderbilt University, 1956) 67-69; Norton,
Struggling for Recognition, 131-32; Williams, "Chaplaincy," 31, 34; and Rufus B. Spain, *At
Ease in Zion: A Social History of the Southern Baptists, 1865-1900* (Nashville: Vanderbilt
University Press, 1967) 33-34.

[26]*Official Records*, series 4, 1:129-30, 252, 275; *Southern Historical Society Papers* 50
(1953): 223-224; and Norton, *Struggling for Recognition*, 132.

judge was characteristic of what some leaders thought about the usefulness of religion on a day-to-day basis in the public sphere. He remarked that chaplains should not expect to be paid as much as regular army officers, for unlike officers who worked every day, ministers performed their jobs only once a week. Many Southern clergy, of course, expressed their resentment at the refusal of their government to support their activities in the army. After the Congress tried to justify its decision to cut the chaplains' salaries as a measure of economy, a writer to the Episcopal *Southern Churchman* inquired disingenuously whether the pay of other soldiers had been similarly reduced. Since officers were paid the same as before, the correspondent remarked sarcastically that the official concern about economy began and ended with the chaplains.[27]

The efforts of the Confederate government to provide financial support for its military chaplaincy improved only slightly as the war progressed. Despite a later increase of the chaplains' pay to $80 a month in 1862, this figure was neither equal to the salary originally allowed to Confederate chaplains, nor close to the $120 then paid to Union chaplains. When the Confederate Congress also enacted legislation that let chaplains draw the rations of a private, it intended this act to be a gesture of generosity towards the clergy. Many ministers, though, considered its provisions to be insulting and a slur against the value of their ministry. The desultory manner in which the Southern government supported its chaplains seemed as problematic for most clergy as the initial refusal to organize a chaplaincy at all.[28]

The failure of Confederate military and civilian officials to provide adequate assistance to chaplains insured that there simply would not be a large enough supply of clergy in the army. As Presbyterian chaplain Robert Lewis Dabney wrote to his wife, the "villainous proceeding" regarding his salary "very much tempted [him] to throw up in disgust" and quit his chaplaincy. Dabney's reaction was certainly typical, for by the spring of 1862, more than half of the Southern regiments lacked chaplains. Stone-

---

[27]*Official Records*, series 4, 1:129-30, 327; Norton, *Struggling for Recognition*, 133; *The Church Intelligencer* 2 (1861): 636, 692; and ibid., 4 (1863): 133. The pay scale in the Confederate army at this time was as follows: brigadier-general ($301/month); surgeon ($200/month); colonel ($195/month); lieutenant-colonel ($170/month); major ($150/month); assistant surgeon ($150/month); captain ($130/month); first lieutenant ($90/month); second lieutenant ($80/month). Chaplains, therefore, were paid lower than all officers, though their pay well exceeded the $13 to $34 per month that enlisted men received; see *Official Records*, series 4, 1:129-30.

[28]*Official Records*, series 4, 1:595, 1076.

wall Jackson, the most pious of all the generals, had entreated the General Assembly of his own Presbyterian Church to send clergy to the Army of Northern Virginia. Jackson himself, though, could not induce ministers to remain in the army with him; by March 1863, only forty-four out of the ninety-one regiments in his corps employed chaplains. [29]

In the armies operating in the western theater of the war, matters were in even worse shape. Several Confederate brigades there were reported to be entirely without chaplains. General Leonidas Polk's corps, for example, had only fifteen out of its forty regiments supplied with chaplains. Clergy in the Army of Tennessee became so discouraged that they contemplated a mass resignation in protest against the apparent indifference of their government to the religious needs of the soldiers and their own efforts to minister to them. These chaplains wanted to believe that they could have an effect on their nation's war effort, but the Confederacy seemed determined to demonstrate that religion had no positive contribution to make to the cause of Southern independence. [30]

Not every Confederate chaplain, of course, was a disgruntled complainer, and some—despite difficult circumstances—tried to do the best they could. The Rev. William E. Wiatt, a thirty-five-year-old Baptist minister, was one of these. He enlisted as a private in the 26th Virginia in 1861, and soon thereafter he was elected its chaplain. Serving the entire length of the war, he visited at least two companies in his regiment every day, passed out Bibles and religious tracts, called on sick and wounded soldiers, and preached regularly. Wiatt kept a diary in which he noted the nature of the church services he led and recorded pertinent information regarding the spiritual state of each man in his regiment. In 1863 and 1864, he also led revivals, during which more than 200 soldiers (nearly half the unit) joined the regimental Christian association. This revival took all

---

[29]Robert Lewis Dabney to his wife, from Manassas VA, 5 September 1861, in the Robert Lewis Dabney Papers, Southern Historical Collection, Library of the University of North Carolina at Chapel Hill; *The Religious Herald* 37 (21 October 1864): 2; William W. Bennett, *A Narrative of the Great Revival Which Prevailed in the Southern Armies During the Late Civil War Between the States of the Federal Union* (Philadelphia: Claxton, Remsen & Haffelfinger, 1877) 51-53; and Francis M. Kennedy, diary entry, 16 March 1863, in the Francis M. Kennedy Papers, Southern Historical Collection, Library of the University of North Carolina at Chapel Hill.

[30]Gorrell Clinton Prim, Jr., "Born Again in the Trenches: Revivalism in the Confederate Army" (Ph.D. diss., Florida State University, 1982) 143-45; W. J. Bennett to Charles Todd Quintard, from Shelbyville TN, 25 March 1863, in the Charles Todd Quintard Papers, Manuscript Department, Duke University Library, Durham NC; and Moses Drury Hoge to W. P. Miles, from Richmond, 7 March 1862, in the Hoge Papers, Richmond.

Wiatt's attention, and he noted with pleasure that the chapel of his brigade was filled daily with new and attentive worshippers. Although he occasionally felt discouraged that he could not accomplish all he wished, he was satisfied with the overall religious situation in the regiment. To him it was a "blessed comfort" to know that his work in the army was "instrumental in honouring God." Wiatt was committed to spreading the gospel among the troops for the benefit of their souls and the moral strength of the Confederacy.[31]

Although Wiatt believed that his proper role should be only as a pastor and never carried arms, many other Southern clergy felt burdened by a sense that they were really needed in battle. The government did nothing to relieve these feelings, but instead seemed to encourage this uneasiness. Despite the fact that ministers were officially exempted from conscription, those who had enlisted as soldiers were (from 1863 on) not allowed to transfer to the chaplaincy of their regiment, if that position became vacant. The reason for that refusal was that every man was then needed as a fighter. In a similar fashion, theological students were always eligible for the draft; the depletion of the student bodies of Southern seminaries and the protests of church leaders did nothing to dissuade the president and his secretary of war from following the course of forcing as many men as possible into the army.[32]

Some comments by clergy who served with the Confederate troops give a picture of the pressures that these men faced. William S. Lacy, a Presbyterian, for instance, enlisted while he was still a seminarian. His professors urged him not to join the army until he was either licensed as a minister or drafted by the government, but Lacy himself "could not shake off the conviction" that duty called him to enter the army as a common soldier. Episcopal clergyman William Nelson Pendleton, who was a graduate of West Point, thought he had to accept the offer of the captaincy of an artillery company. He could not refuse to become an artillery officer, he wrote, without "injuring religion . . . by allowing some to infer that the Gospel hope adds little to courage,—and actually denying prayer." James K. Street enlisted as a private in the 9th Texas Regiment, but he was not allowed to apply for the chaplaincy of that unit when the post be-

---

[31]James I. Robertson, Jr., "Chaplain William E. Wiatt: Soldier of the Cloth," in *Rank and File: Civil War Essays in Honor of Bell Irvin Wiley*, ed. James I. Robertson, Jr., and Richard M. McMurry (San Rafael CA: Presidio Press, 1976) 113-20, 123-27, 131-32.

[32]*Official Records*, series 4, 1:723, 1081; ibid., series 4, 3:179; Norton, "Organization and Function," 67-69; and W. Harrison Daniel, "The Effects of the Civil War on Southern Protestantism," *Maryland Historical Magazine* 69 (1974): 53.

came available. He later was accepted as the chaplain of the 14th Texas only after an ankle injury made him unfit for further service in battle. And Mark Perrin Lowrey, a clergyman who worked both as a brigadier-general and as a Baptist missionary, said that he agreed with the official decision to keep clergy in the ranks of the soldiers. Lowrey was convinced that the churches at home really did not want their pastors to stay aloof from the wartime crisis, but thought that every able-bodied man "should rise and stand between his home and the enemy."[33]

Certainly, clergymen might have been used to augment the depleted Confederate army, but were they needed in the way that Lowrey thought they were? There is a good deal of evidence to suggest that most South-erners did not want to see chaplains and ministers taking part in the kill-ing of other men. When Leonidas Polk laid aside his duties as the Episcopal bishop of Louisiana and accepted a military commission, for instance, *The Church Intelligencer* stated that this action had shocked the majority of Southern Christians. The editors acknowledged that patriotism moti-vated many clergymen like Polk to become soldiers and find a "wider field of usefulness" in that role, but the editors urged them to seek that useful-ness in the office of chaplain, which was the "right and proper" position for a clergyman. Bishop Stephen Elliott, Polk's colleague in the diocese of Georgia, wrote Polk to say that the clergy he knew disapproved of Polk's action. Although Elliott himself called that decision "defensible" under the circumstances of the war, he also feared that Polk was going to have to bear the brunt of much criticism. J. H. Ticknor, another friend of Polk, said that he was "startled" that Polk had entered the army. Ticknor (as Elliott had done) assured Polk that he himself approved of what had hap-pened, yet he too conceded that even Polk's admirers thought it "wrong under almost any other imaginable circumstances."[34]

---

[33]William S. Lacy to his mother, from Gordonsville VA, 19 March 1862, in the Drury Lacy Papers, Southern Historical Collection, Library of the University of North Carolina at Chapel Hill; William Nelson Pendleton, personal note, 1 May 1861, in the William Nelson Pendleton Papers, Southern Historical Collection, Library of the University of North Carolina at Chapel Hill; James K. Street to his wife from the camp of Co. "A," 9th Texas Regiment, 28 October 1863, in the James K. Street Papers, Southern Historical Collection, Library of the University of North Carolina at Chapel Hill; and Mark Perrin Lowrey, "An Autobiography," *Southern Historical Society Papers* 16 (1888): 368.

[34]*The Church Intelligencer* 2 (1861): 501, 533, 550; Stephen Elliott to Leonidas Polk, from Savannah, 6 August 1861, in the Leonidas Polk Papers, Jessie Ball DuPont Library, University of the South, Sewanee TN; and J. H. Ticknor to Leonidas Polk, from Selma AL, 22 July 1861, in the Polk Papers, Sewanee.

Leonidas Polk, Episcopal bishop of Louisiana and lieutenant-general, C.S.A.
(photograph courtesy of the University of the South).

Other churchmen criticized clergy who raised troops or accepted commissions in the army. The *Tennessee Baptist* expressed distress at hearing that Robert Lewis Dabney, a well-known Presbyterian, had left the chaplaincy to become a staff officer for Stonewall Jackson, and *The Religious Herald* declared its conviction that a chaplain's duties ought to be entirely spiritual. In a like manner, Stonewall Jackson rebuked a chaplain who advanced into the battleline. Jackson believed that chaplains belonged in the rear of the army where they could attend to the work to which they

FANCY SKETCH OF RIGHT REVEREND MAJOR-GENERAL BISHOP POLK HEADING HIS "DIVISION."

A Northern caricature of Leonidas Polk (Harper's Weekly 5 [1861]: 467).

had properly been called. All Jackson wanted his chaplains to do was pray for the success of the Southern cause.[35]

The consensus in the Southern churches was that clergy who took up arms were failing to obey their high calling from God, for ministers should be concerned only with saving sinners and never with killing them. Clergymen who used weapons, moreover, defied the cultural norm dictating that the spiritual and ecclesiastical sphere ought to be entirely separate from the secular and political one. Southern ministers may have hoped to identify themselves with the plight of their people by fighting on their behalf, but in so doing they violated one of the cardinal doctrines on which Southern culture was based: the notion of privatized religion. The most useful contributions the Southern church could make, it seemed, were spiritual and not temporal.

Clergy who served in the Civil War armies—North as well as South—were torn between competing and sometimes contradictory expectations regarding their behavior. Activities that might win the respect and admiration of one particular regiment might well offend other men, and chaplains could never be sure if they were functioning in the right capacity at the right time with the right people. Some of the chaplains' problems, of course, were common to all American clergy and reflected an anticlerical bias often found in American religion. Clergymen usually gained approval not because of their ecclesiastical standing as such, but rather by their willingness to undertake informal, practical duties that helped their men. The hesitance of the Union and Confederate governments to specify the ministers' military role was indicative in part of larger issues in the uneasy relationship between the churches and the surrounding culture.

There were, on the other hand, clear differences between the ways in which clergy were treated in the Northern and Southern armies. While the Union government recognized immediately the need to support a military chaplaincy among its troops, Confederate leaders at first hoped that no formal chaplaincy would be necessary at all. The Northern govern-

---

[35]W. Harrison Daniel, "Protestantism and Patriotism in the Confederacy," *Mississippi Quarterly* 24 (1971): 123-24; Frank L. Hieronymous, "For Now and Forever: The Chaplains of the Confederate States Army" (Ph.D. diss., University of California at Los Angeles, 1964) 49-50; Norton, *Struggling for Recognition*, 158; and Oscar P. Fitzgerald, *John B. McFerrin: A Biography* (Nashville: Publishing House of the M. E. Church, South, 1888) 278, 341.

ment, moreover, expected that the clergy whom it employed would be responsible for overseeing the moral health of their units. Southerners tended to shy away from that assumption, and they provided neither overt support for the chaplaincy nor any specific directions about what chaplains should do. Soldiers, not ministers, were what the Confederacy seemed to need the most. Yet when clergymen tested that assumption and tried to be useful as armed soldiers, those attempts were also viewed with disapproval by many of their countrymen. Southern ministers soon learned that their enthusiasm for military service would be largely unappreciated by their own people and that, consequently, their contribution to the war effort of their nation could be tenuous at best.

One Baptism of Blood: Army Revivals and Northern Victory

4

Writing in the latter stages of the war about his experiences as chaplain of the 63rd Pennsylvania Regiment, James Marks highlighted the work he had undertaken in leading revivals among the Northern soldiers early in 1862. In Marks's mind, that had been a miserable time for his men and other troops then encamped near Washington. Bitterness and shock from the defeat at Bull Run gripped the Union army during the prolonged period of inactivity after the battle. The weather was cold, wet, and muddy, and homesickness and a general ennui were the most common feelings of the soldiers. Marks decided that, rather than allowing the men to wallow in their unhappiness, he would instead bring their thoughts to "those truths which have ever stilled the tumult of human passion." He bought a tent for public worship, and soon "hundreds" in the camp with his regiment participated in a revival season that lasted until the army left Washington during the Peninsula campaign in the spring. Not only had the revival provided spiritual comfort for soldiers about to face death in battle, Marks thought, but it also gave them psychological relief from the discomforts of their winter encampment. The soldiers had been imbued with discipline and purpose, and they were prepared to confront the further hardships of army life.[1]

Revivals like Marks described were not usually among the first experiences of the men who entered the Union army in 1861. Although the bloodshed and indecision of that year sobered many in the North, to most new soldiers the war still seemed to be a lighthearted adventure, and the

[1]James Marks, *The Peninsular Campaign in Virginia, or Incidents and Scenes on the Battle-Fields and in Richmond* (Philadelphia: J. B. Lippincott & Co., 1864) 54-60.

excitement at beginning military service prevented them from giving much sustained attention to religious matters. Religious observances—such as they were—were limited to Sunday preaching, occasional weekday prayer meetings, and the private devotions of especially pious soldiers. However, revivalistic activity did slowly develop; revivals began sporadically in 1862 in large encampments at Washington, Chicago, and St. Louis where Northern troops were gathering and training.[2]

The boredom of camp life prior to the spring campaigns of 1862 was probably the greatest moral obstacle facing Union soldiers at that time. The days passed slowly with little real work to do, and as a consequence men were often tempted to "make some foolishness together" (as one soldier described it). Profanity, drunkenness, licentiousness, gambling, and petty thievery seemed to confront those who wanted to practice their faith in the army. General Robert McAllister, for example, complained to his wife that a "tide of irreligion" had rolled over his army "like a mighty wave." Religious men, he believed, had to guard themselves constantly against the spreading contagion of demoralization engendered by their fellow soldiers. Christians often were forced to associate with irreligious men who mocked the faith they held and prevented them from engaging in prayer and meditation on the scriptures.[3]

One of the greatest complaints of evangelicals concerned the failure of the army to set aside Sunday for rest or church services. As a private noted in his diary, "there is Sunday in the almanac but in military affairs there seems to be no sacred day." Instead of giving themselves to the worship of God, he wrote, soldiers were "playing cards[,] swearing and dancing just as on other days." Many soldiers felt out of place in the regular routines of army service and thought that Sunday actually was the hardest working day of the week. Officers seemed to consider the Sabbath as a time for inspections of their units or for parading their men. Such activities, while surely not intended as an outright affront to evangelicals in the North, had a disruptive effect on men who were accustomed to keeping a Sabbath rest at home.[4]

---

[2]United States Christian Commission, *Annual Report* 1 (1862): 96-99.

[3]Henry A. Kircher, *A German in the Yankee Fatherland: The Civil War Letters of Henry A. Kircher*, ed. Earl J. Hess (Kent OH: Kent State University Press, 1983) 11-12, 16; Robert McAllister, *The Civil War Letters of General Robert McAllister*, ed. James I. Robertson, Jr. (New Brunswick NJ: Rutgers University Press, 1965) 103; and John William DeForest, *A Volunteer's Adventures: A Union Captain's Record of the Civil War*, ed. James H. Croushore (New Haven: Yale University Press, 1946) 43, 65.

[4]Cyrus F. Boyd, *The Civil War Diary of Cyrus F. Boyd: Fifteenth Iowa Infantry, 1861-*

Religious services in camp: Chaplain Drake preaching to the 31st Ohio Regiment at Camp Dick Rubinson, Kentucky, 10 November 1861 (photograph courtesy of the Library of Congress).

In response to this situation, General George B. McClellan resolved early in the war that his men would not work on the Sabbath if at all possible. Having experienced a religious conversion soon after his appointment to the command of the Army of the Potomac, McClellan ordered in September 1861 that the "holy cause" in which the North was engaged required Sabbath observances in camp and that divine services should be held on every Sunday morning that military necessity did not absolutely prevent such worship. Among McClellan's subordinates at the time, General Oliver O. Howard (known thoughout the nation as "the Christian soldier") was the most supportive of this decision. Because the observance of the Sabbath was a fundamental tenet of the faith of the American people, Howard reasoned, it ought to be respected by military leaders. Violation of the Sabbath only weakened the spirit of soldiers who were strong and convinced Christians, and the fact that the Federal army had attacked on a Sunday morning had been one of the causes of the defeat at First Bull Run. Howard wrote in his postwar memoirs that McClellan's order had assured that God's blessings would rest upon the Union cause; at that moment, ultimate victory for the North became a certainty.[5]

Howard had been converted in 1857 after reading the diary of Hedley Vicars, the noted British evangelical soldier. Howard briefly studied for the ministry, and although the outbreak of the Civil War permanently deferred his interest in a ministerial career, he still sought opportunities in the army to exercise his religious calling. As a brigade commander, Howard made sure that each of his regiments held services on Sunday, and if no chaplain were present in a regiment, Howard officiated at its services. A soldier who heard Howard preach commented favorably on the "eloquent addresses and earnest exhortations" that he delivered. That soldier was gratified to know that Howard, "though he ranked high among men, . . . humbled himself before God."[6]

1863, ed. Mildred Throne (Millwood NY: Kraus Reprint Co., 1977) 23-24; and Charles M. Clark, The History of the Thirty-Ninth Regiment, Illinois Volunteer Infantry (Chicago: Veteran Association of the Regiment, 1889) 95-96.

[5]George B. McClellan, McClellan's Own Story: The War for the Union (New York: Charles L. Webster and Company, 1887) 355, 395, 402, 445; Methodist Quarterly Review 44 (1862): 467-68; and Oliver O. Howard, Autobiography of Oliver Otis Howard, Major General United States Army (Freeport NY: Books for Libraries Press, 1971) 1:164-65.

[6]Oliver O. Howard, Major-General Howard's Address at the Second Anniversary of the U. S. Christian Commission (Philadelphia: Caxton Press, 1864) 10-11; William S. McFeely, Yankee Stepfather: General O. O. Howard and the Freedmen (New Haven: Yale University Press, 1968) 38; John A. Carpenter, Sword and Olive Branch: Oliver Otis Howard (Pittsburgh: University of Pittsburgh Press, 1964) 30; and Bell Irvin Wiley, The Life of Billy Yank: The Common Soldier of the Union (Indianapolis: The Bobbs-Merrill Co., 1952) 268.

In the western theater, William Rosecrans was another prominent general who promoted the spiritual interests of his men. When he took over the leadership of the Army of the Ohio in the fall of 1862, for example, he increased the number of chaplains serving in the regiments under his command. Rosecrans also made a policy never to fight on Sundays, and he followed that dictum scrupulously even though it was apparently detrimental to his military success. Thus, at Murfreesboro he refused to pursue his beaten foe on the Sunday after that battle and chose instead to give his army a Sabbath rest. He vowed that his army would rely wholly on God, who, he said, "never fails those who truly trust."[7]

Sunday services at General McClellan's headquarters (*Harper's Weekly* 6 [1862]: 517).

---

[7]William M. Lamers, *The Edge of Glory: A Biography of General William S. Rosecrans, U. S. A.* (New York: Harcourt, Brace & World, Inc., 1961) 188, 242, 338; and James Lee

General Oliver O. Howard, "the Christian soldier" (photograph courtesy of the Library of Congress).

McDonough, *Chattanooga—A Death Grip on the Confederacy* (Knoxville: The University of Tennessee Press, 1984) 45.

As a Roman Catholic, however, Rosecrans came under criticism from many Protestants who feared that his religious concerns amounted to little more than pessimistic fatalism. Government officals such as Charles A. Dana, the Assistant Secretary of War, interpreted Rosecrans's overt acts of piety as a sign that the army was actually "in a desperate situation." After the almost disastrous loss at Chickamauga and Rosecrans's removal from high command, moreover, the *New York Times* reported that the defeat had been caused by his proclivity to profound religious depression. He was allegedly so paralyzed by his dependence on divine initiative that he was unable to take an energetic role in the deployment and use of his troops. Although the accuracy of the report made by the *Times* is certainly questionable, its accusation does reveal the qualities that mainline Protestants were seeking in the military leaders of their nation. Northerners were looking for an activistic, optimistic faith—a faith that would inspire soldiers to be victorious and not just console them when they were beaten.[8]

Revivalism, in fact, was to supply that needed quality that boosted the morale of the Northern army. At the midpoint of the war, the spirits of the troops were invigorated by the decisive victories at Gettysburg, Vicksburg, and Chattanooga, and the revivals following those battles would further inspire the confidence of the Union soldiers. The gradual emergence of revivalism in the armies in 1863 suggests that the tested Northern veterans were turning from their original carefree attitude about the war toward a more reflective, religious stance. Revivals began to occur in the spring and summer and gained strength as the soldiers entered winter quarters at the end of the year. As the significance of the recent military triumphs became apparent in the North, the Union forces seemed to gather themselves together—spiritually as well as materially—for the intensified onslaught against the South.[9]

In the Army of the Potomac, a great religious excitement appeared during the winter of 1863-1864 as many brigades built churches and chapel tents for prayer meetings. In February 1864, a Christian Commission agent

---

[8]Lamers, *Edge of Glory*, 401; McDonough, *Chattanooga*, 8, 44-45; and George Templeton Strong, *The Diary of George Templeton Strong*, ed. Allan Nevins and Milton Halsey Thomas (New York: The Macmillan Co., 1952)3: 366.

[9]Leonard Moss, *Annals of the United States Christian Commission* (Philadelphia: J. B. Lippincott & Co., 1868) 377, 400-401; Christian Commission, *Annual Report* 2 (1863): 37-38; ibid., 3 (1864): 28, 66-67; and McAllister, *Civil War Letters*, 286-87, 329.

recorded in his diary that a period of unusual spiritual interest had begun in the army, and brigade chapels were so full that some men were not able to come inside to join in prayer. General McAllister, who was then working closely with the Christian Commission, wrote to his wife that he had never seen "a better state of feeling in religious matters" in the Army of the Potomac. A report in the *American Missionary* of May 1864 spoke with pleasure concerning religious events among the Union soldiers, hoped that both the army and the whole nation would be converted by them, and reasoned that no foe could stand before such an army of Christian officers and men.[10]

The men of the 61st New York Regiment forming a hollow square for worship (Harper's Weekly 6 [1862]: 281).

---

[10]Diary of the Christian Commission delegate at Nelson Station, Warrenton VA, 14 February-20 March 1864, and report of an agent from Stoneman's Switch, Falmouth VA, 28 March 1864, in the United States Christian Commission Records, Record Group 94, item nos. 757 and 794, National Archives, Washington DC; McAllister, *Civil War Letters*, 401; *American Missionary* 8 (1864): 124; Emory M. Stevens, "Story of the Chaplain,"

At the same time, religious interest began to peak in the Department of the South, and especially among black troops serving in garrisons along the Atlantic coast. White missionaries who worked with those troops reported the presence of "a subdued feeling—a chastened submission to the will of God" in their camps. Soldiers were beginning to realize that God was indeed going to bless their struggle for freedom with success. One minister wrote that his men had acknowledged the divine "plan of mercy, of freedom—of purity for the nation," and that as a result of this acceptance of God's will, "a spiritual vision seem[ed] to be coming over the army." Although those soldiers were not destined to have a role in the major offensives that ended the war, they did share the spiritual fervor inspiring all the Union forces as the great military crises of 1863 were favorably passed.[11]

The greatest revival of this period took place in the West in the early fall of 1863. Leonard Moss, writing after the war about the work of the United States Christian Commission, believed that this revival gained its special strength from the close proximity of the bloody defeat at Chickamauga in September to the victory at Chattanooga two months later. The soldiers who survived the awful ordeal of Chickamauga were so shaken by their experience, he said, that they felt more profoundly than ever the need to accept Jesus as their Savior. The arrival of U. S. Grant as commander of the Union troops in Chattanooga also renewed the soldiers' desire to fight. Religious enthusiasm and military morale were revived simultaneously, thereby preparing the men for their most astounding victory of the war: the storming of Lookout Mountain and Missionary Ridge.[12]

Some Northerners viewed the rout of the Confederate forces at Chattanooga as not only a spectacular military achievement, but also as an act of God undertaken on behalf of the Federal cause. The men who watched the Union soldiers overrun the Southern position on Missionary Ridge, for example, at first could not believe what they saw. It was so unexpected and sudden that soldiers after the war thought that charge had been the

---

in *The Story of Our Regiment: A History of the 148th Pennsylvania Vols*, ed. J. W. Muffly (Des Moines IA: The Kenyon Printing & Mfg. Co., 1904) 195; and Wilbur Fisk, *Anti-Rebel: The Civil War Letters of Wilbur Fisk* (Croton-on-Hudson NY: Emil Rosenblatt, 1983) 200-201.

[11]Willie Lee Rose, *Rehearsal for Reconstruction: The Port Royal Experiment* (Indianapolis: The Bobbs-Merrill Company, 1964) 262-63.

[12]Moss, *Annals*, 468-70; Moses D. Gage, *From Vicksburg to Raleigh; or, A Complete History of the Twelfth Regiment Indiana Volunteer Infantry* (Chicago: Clarke & Co., 1865) 113-14; and James M. McPherson, *Ordeal by Fire: The Civil War and Reconstruction* (New York: Alfred A. Knopf, 1982) 339.

most dramatic of the conflict. Charles Dana declared that it ranked among "the greatest miracles in military history" and was "a visible interposition of God" for the Union. General John W. Geary, who had been involved in the attack on nearby Lookout Mountain, had a similar comment about his own part in the battle. "I have been the instrument of Almighty God," he wrote in an exultant letter to his wife, for he believed that his soldiers had accomplished what should have been—by any human standard—an impossible task.[13]

Having broken the siege at Chattanooga and rejoicing in a triumph that seemed unattainable just a few weeks before, the Northern army encamped at Ringgold, Georgia, for the winter. The revival that had started in Chattanooga continued at Ringgold, and during this time hundreds of new converts were baptized in Chickamauga Creek. For the men who were veterans of the battlefield through which the creek flowed, immersion in the Chickamauga gave a profound, spiritual meaning to the chaos of the battle they had survived. Just as the battle of Chickamauga had been both a terrible defeat for the Union army and a preparation for the stunning victory at Chattanooga, so the river itself became for those troops not only a fearsome place of death, but also a symbol of their death to the old life of sin and rebirth to new life in Jesus Christ. These revivals at Ringgold united the soldiers emotionally and readied them corporately for the next campaign against the Confederates.[14]

Several visitors to the camp at this time noted that there was a spirit in evidence that had not been present before. Soldiers were enthusiastically worshipping together without regard for denominational lines; they rallied themselves around the same cross as well as the same flag. A missionary of the American Tract Society spoke insightfully about the connection between the revival and the army's upcoming offensive. The men, he observed, united under

> one Lord, one faith, one baptism, . . . were all going down to the one baptism of blood; they were all to take the one cup of suffering; and many were to go into the church invisible . . . before many suns had risen and set.

---

[13]McDonough, *Chattanooga*, 142, 167.

[14]Moss, *Annals*, 490-91, 498-500; Albion W. Tourgee, *The Story of a Thousand, Being a History of the Service of the 105th Ohio Volunteer Infantry* (Buffalo: S. McGerald and Son, 1896) 390; Edward Parmelee Smith, *Incidents of the United States Christian Commission* (Philadelphia: Lippincott & Co., 1869) 277-78; and Albertus A. Dunham and Charles LaForest Dunham, *Through the South with a Union Soldier*, ed. Arthur H. DeRosier, Jr. (Johnson City: The East Tennessee State University, 1969) 116.

Revivals and the military experiences of the soldiers, therefore, were proving to be mutually supportive. Each provided the other with a significance and interpretation that impelled the men forward with renewed fervor on their way to ultimate victory.[15]

The army revivals of 1861-1865 did not arise in isolation from other religious trends in America. They were, in fact, part of a greater revivalistic movement at work throughout the nineteenth century. The revivals in the Civil War armies were linked most closely to the so-called "businessman's" revival of 1857, which had begun in several major cities and then spread throughout the country just prior to the war. Many of the officials of the United States Christian Commission had been active leaders in the earlier revival—George Stuart, the president of the Commission, and William E. Boardman, its executive secretary, being the most prominent. For them and others like them, the excitement of the army revival was simply a continuation of what had already begun in 1857.[16]

The revival of 1857-1858, ecumenical and lay in emphasis, had affected all classes and regions, and as the testimony of many Civil War participants reveals, men who were converted in the prewar revivals carried their faith and enthusiasm with them into the army. The effects of the prewar revival had been felt in the army whenever new recruits organized Christian associations and prayer meetings like those they had had at home. A Christian Commission tract made note of this fact near the end of the war. The authors of that tract claimed that men who had been converted in the 1857-1858 revival resolved not to leave their religion behind them, but to practice it faithfully when they entered the army. In the minds of the participants in the revivals, of course, there was no arbitrary division between their religious experiences before and after 1861. The mere outbreak of a conflict even as momentous as the Civil War could not prevent Christian soldiers from feeling the presence of their Lord with them.[17]

---

[15]*Western Christian Advocate* 31 (1864): 83; and American Tract Society, New England Branch, *Annual Report* 5 (1864): 21.

[16]Leonard I. Sweet, " 'A Nation Born Again': The Union Prayer Meeting Revival and Cultural Revitalization," in *In the Great Tradition: Themes Honoring the Writings of Winthrop S. Hudson*, ed. Joseph D. Ban (Valley Forge PA: Judson Press, 1982) 194-201, 212-13.

[17]*Christ in the Army: A Selection of Sketches of the Work of the U. S. Christian Commission* (Philadelphia: Ladies' Christian Commission, 1865) 17; and Cornelius H. Edgar, "Germs and Growth," in *Render Unto Caesar: A Collection of Sermon Classics on All Phases of Religion in Wartime* (New York: Lewis Publishing Company, 1943) 78-79.

The revivals of 1857-1858 and 1863-1865, moreover, had several other common emphases. Most visible of these was the relative absence of women in the businessman's revival, in which the percentage of males converted was larger than in any other nineteenth-century revival, except those in the Civil War armies. Men who were active in religious gatherings in 1857 became accustomed to seeing a predominantly male group, and male-dominated revivals naturally continued in the army. The revival before the war was also notable for the way in which it blurred the distinctions between laymen and clergy in its membership. Lay leadership remained important in the army revivals because of both the relative lack of clergy and the belief that traditional ecclesiastical distinctions were without justification in the informal setting of camp life. Those who organized revivals in the Union army intentionally encouraged leadership and participation by as large a group of soldiers as possible.[18]

The revivals operated on the most basic level of belief—the lowest common denominator—on which evangelicals of every denomination could find agreement. Fine theological distinctions were of no interest to most soldiers. Thus, when a Union officer commented on a communion service involving Presbyterians, Methodists, Baptists, and Congregationalists and observed the "strange" and "pleasant" harmony existing among them all, he recognized that army life had occasioned a significant alteration of the usual ecclesiastical procedures. Those who took part in the revivals were not concerned with theoretical issues of theology or church polity, but simply with the experience of conversion and dedication to Christian living. In this regard, the army revivals were quintessentially American, that is, laying stress more on participation and practicality than on contemplation and speculation. The leaders of the revivals were concerned more with *results* than with process.[19]

Chaplains and missionaries claimed that most men who were active in the army revivals remained committed church members after the war and brought back with them the pious emotions they had experienced in the camp. Although the Civil War had been expected to deal as disastrous a blow to organized religion as the American Revolution had, the continuation of religious interest in the army convinced church leaders that they

---

[18]Sweet, " 'A Nation Born Again,' " 194, 204; and Frank Milton Bristol, *The Life of Chaplain McCabe, Bishop of the Methodist Episcopal Church* (New York: Fleming H. Revell, Co., 1908) 160.

[19]McAllister, *Civil War Letters*, 405; and Newton Martin Curtis, *From Bull Run to Chancellorsville: The Story of the Sixteenth New York Infantry Together with Personal Reminiscences* (New York: G. P. Putnam's Sons, 1906) 211.

had little cause for worry. Some chaplains even thought they had seen more conversions in their regiments in a few months than they had ever seen in their civilian pastorates. Lemuel Moss of the Christian Commission asserted that religious events in the Northern armies had made a minister's labors outside military circles appear "formal and fruitless," and he was delighted that most of the Commission's delegates had carried the spirit of the army revivals to their parishioners at home.[20]

The continuing closeness and threat of death also forced thousands of soldiers to reflect on God's control over human destinies and enabled them

A Bible class in a Union artillery unit (Christian Commission, *Annual Report* 2 [1863]: opposite title page).

---

[20]Moss, *Annals*, 180, 575-76; Ekman, "Northern Religion and the Civil War" (Ph. D. diss., Harvard University, 1972) 154-55; United States Christian Commission, *Christian Commission for the Army and Navy of the United States of America* (Philadelphia: Ringwalt & Brown, 1862) 9; and James H. Moorhead, *American Apocalypse: Yankee Protestants and the Civil War, 1860-1869* (New Haven: Yale University Press, 1978) 71.

to turn to religion for meaning in the midst of the events of the war. As a
letter from a soldier in the 129th Michigan stated in its homely fashion,

> Iff thare is any place that a person ought to lade a criston life heare is the
> place, for a person dont know what time he will be cald up for to leave
> this world of trouble.

The suddenness and unexpectedness of casualties prevented any man from
thinking that *he* was master of his fate. Since stray bullets and cannon balls
often struck down the unwary, those dangers convinced many men that
God's inscrutable providence alone protected their souls and bodies. "I
prayed on the battle field some of the best prayers I ever prayed in my life,"
one black soldier admitted. The battlefield was "the valley and the shadow
of death" to Christians, but they obtained some sense of mastery over its
dangers by surrendering their claim to autonomy, acknowledging God's
transcendent power, and linking their wills to the divine will.[21]

Most Northerners were convinced that revivalism occupied an unusually useful position in the context of army life. Men who were religious
and who had shared in the revivals were thought to be better soldiers, more
disciplined, and more accepting of hardships than those who were not religious. Christians were said to stand firm in battle, while "unconverted"
regiments broke and ran at threatening moments. Religious beliefs had
calmed the fears of many soldiers and helped them function bravely as
warriors, confident that their lives were under God's care. Oliver Howard, for instance, described a depression and paralysis that gripped him right
before he entered the fighting. He always engaged in prayer, he said, in
order to counteract those feelings. Praying not only seemed to maintain
his courage, but also provided him with "a feeling akin to gaiety" when
the battle surrounded him.[22]

Newton Martin Curtis, another religious Union officer, wrote after the
war about the sensations he felt while under enemy fire. Curtis claimed
that, although most soldiers were nervous before a battle, the activities in
which they engaged helped to make them temporarily heedless of the dangers they faced. The fighting spawned unselfish men who, rather than
fearing injury, worried instead that their conduct might discredit them in

---

[21]Dunham, *Through the South,* 134; Leon F. Litwack, *Been in the Storm So Long: The
Aftermath of Slavery* (New York: Alfred A. Knopf, 1979) 100; and Boyd, *Civil War Diary,*
39.

[22]"Christianity in the Army," *The Christian Register* 47 (11 July 1868): 2; and [Elizabeth
A. W. Dwight], *Life and Letters of Wilder Dwight, Lieut-Col. Second Mass. Inf. Vols.* (Boston: Ticknor and Fields, 1868) 271, 293.

the eyes of those who fought beside them. Battle made them turn away from their everyday concerns and work for the benefit of their comrades, their units, and their nation. Curtis was certain, therefore, that the war had had a positive influence on the personalities of the majority of men who fought in it. Despite the arguments of a few who said that war made men more brutish, Curtis thought that battle had actually "refined" and "brightened" the natures of most Civil War soldiers.[23]

Union soldiers often echoed the preaching of their clergymen, who sought to convince soldiers that dying in battle with a clear conscience and in defense of a righteous cause would provide them entrance into the heavenly kingdom. Thus, men who were converted in the army revivals imagined that their ultimate reward was martyrdom, and they commonly employed that image to describe the deaths of their pious comrades. When sergeant Ira Dodd's captain was killed in action, therefore, Dodd called his death "nothing less than martyrdom" and extolled the man as "a noble Christian, the light of whose example shone ever with bright and benignant ray." Another soldier linked the deaths of his fellow soldiers directly to the national crusade against slavery. He feared that some of his countrymen might not "realize that the Sacrifice of our brave and noble comrads [sic] who have fallen in the Struggle are every one of them martyrs." Using language that echoed Abraham Lincoln's own, this soldier asserted, "Justice demands at our hands that they shall not have fallen in vain, but that Every vestige of the great National sin: (Slavery) Shall be washed ayway [sic] with their blood."[24]

Black troops, of course, had the clearest perspective on the religious implications of the struggle against slavery. Thomas Wentworth Higginson, colonel of the first regiment raised among freedmen in the South, was deeply impressed by the role religion assumed in his camp. A former Unitarian minister from Massachusetts, Higginson confessed that he did not encourage "the extremes of religious enthusiasm" that revivalism often produced, but he still admired the devotion that his " 'Gospel army' " of black soldiers continually displayed. He recorded anecdotes in his diary about how the faith of the men inspired and emboldened them: " 'Let me lib wid de musket in one hand an' de Bible in de oder, —dat . . . I may know I hab de bressed Jesus in my hand, an' hab no fear,' " one soldier

---

[23]Curtis, From Bull Run to Chancellorsville, 268-71.

[24]Ira S. Dodd, The Song of the Rappahannock: Sketches of the Civil War (New York: Dodd, Mead, and Company, 1898) 158-59; and Joseph T. Glatthaar, The March to the Sea and Beyond: Sherman's Troops in the Savannah and Carolinas Campaigns (New York: New York University Press, 1985) 40.

prayed. Another man referred to his comrades as " 'a chosen people,' " who sought God's blessings as they gathered for prayer. This soldier believed that the war was a " 'great baptism of suffering' " for all who fought on the side of the Union; the suffering they endured on behalf of such a noble cause was a sign of the favor they had found with God.[25]

Social factors also shaped the revivals that sprang up throughout the Union army during the last two years of the war. Symbolizing the gradual development of bonds uniting men in the common experience of military life, religious meetings occurred with increasing frequency as the conflict progressed. For those who were cut off from the ordinary circumstances of life and lived under physical conditions that were harsh and unsettled, religious activities provided a stability often lacking in their environment. This had played a part in the revivals on the frontier earlier in the century, and it continued to be important amid the relatively primitive conditions of the military camps. Revivalism brought a type of discipline, order, and community that even the regulated life of an army in wartime was unable to provide. It linked soldiers both spiritually to the churches at home and emotionally to one another in new associations in the camps.[26]

While the Army of the Potomac had been constantly on the move during the attacks at the Wilderness, Spotsylvania Court House, and Cold Harbor in 1864, the revivals there were brought to a temporary halt. (Maintaining revivals when an army was on an active campaign was extremely difficult, for men who were busy in the field had little chance to organize large-scale religious activities.) But when the troops settled into entrenchments along the Richmond-Petersburg line, interest in revivalism rose dramatically. At City Point on the James River (the headquarters and chief supply area of the Army of the Potomac for the next nine months), prayer meetings remained in progress throughout the summer. Located at the organizational heart of the army, these revivals took place in the midst of the bustle of men and supplies journeying back and forth

---

[25]Thomas Wentworth Higginson, *Army Life in a Black Regiment* (New York: W. W. Norton & Company, 1984) 48, 71, 240-41; and Higginson, journal entries, 12 January 1863 and 13 March 1864, in the Thomas Wentworth Higginson Papers, Houghton Library, Harvard University, Cambridge MA.

[26]For an analysis of the connection between frontier revivalism and social order, see especially Donald Mathews, "The Second Great Awakening as an Organizing Process, 1780-1830," *American Quarterly* 21 (1969): 23-43; and Dickson D. Bruce, Jr., *And They All Sang Hallelujah: Plain-Folk Camp-Meeting Religion, 1800-1845* (Knoxville: The University of Tennessee Press, 1974) 34-35.

between the rear areas and the siege lines. Wherever Union soldiers gathered at this period, whether at City Point in the rear or at brigade chapels built near the front, they were able to participate in revivalistic activities.[27]

From late 1864 until the end of the war, the Northern troops in Virginia were reported to have supported a "pentecostal season" of unsurpassed magnitude. In the Army of the Potomac and the Army of the James, both operating in relatively settled conditions, revivalism reached its peak in the winter and spring of 1865. The prayer meetings were "glorious," one participant noted, as soldiers crowded together to experience the excitement of mass religious conversions. Although a Christian Commission delegate in the XVIII Corps worried that some men were not as serious as they ought to be regarding the commitment they made, even he was excited about the "constant religious interest" that surrounded him. In Tennessee as well, the Union troops defending that state against Confederate thrusts in the winter of 1864-1865 were caught up in a similar revivalistic movement. Union forces everywhere celebrated their approaching victory with not only worldly but also spiritual enthusiasm.[28]

Most impressive of all, perhaps, were the revivals in Sherman's mobile army marching through the Carolinas. Whenever soldiers stopped for the night or encamped for a short period, they gathered in churches they found along the way and gave thanks to God for the successes they had won each day. The Christian association of one brigade in the XX Corps, for example, saw a rapid expansion of its membership in the last few weeks of the war. This association grew from an original 50 men to more than 300, and it welcomed several hundred others as onlookers at its nightly meetings. A large outdoor arena with log benches, an altar, and a pulpit was constructed for the brigade at Goldsboro, North Carolina, but despite the large size of that facility, many still had to stand in the rear to hear the prayers and preaching. In Charleston, South Carolina, the black troops who marched into that city in April 1865 observed the war's end with revivals. They entered the city "singing Methodist hymns," a Charleston resident reported, and their camp meetings created "tremendous excite-

---

[27]Christian Commission, *Annual Report* 3 (1864): 62-67.

[28]Moss, *Annals*, 447; Christian Commission, *Annual Report* 4 (1865): 107-108, 117, 156, 187-88, 191; and diaries of Christian Commission delegates from the V Corps (26 February 1865), the XVIII Corps (19 May 1865), and Wild's Station VA (8 February 1865) in the Christian Commission Records, Record Group 94, item no. 757, Washington.

CHAPEL AT MEADE STATION, VA.—EXTERIOR.

United States Christian Commission chapel erected during revivals in the latter stages of the war (Moss, *Annals*, 182-83).

ment," as the soldiers prayed that "their cause might prosper & their just freedom be obtained."[29]

In the late spring of 1865, the troops of every major Union army assembled near Washington and prepared for the transition from military to civilian status. Knowing that this was the final opportunity to minister to such a large gathering of men, agents of the Christian Commission zealously plunged into the task of saving souls. As a result of these efforts, re-

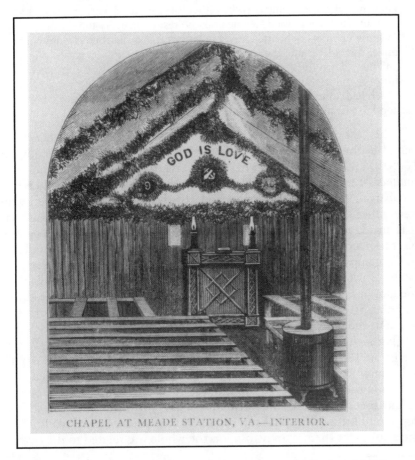

CHAPEL AT MEADE STATION, VA.—INTERIOR.

Interior of the Christian Commission chapel (Moss, *Annals*, 184-85).

[29]Glatthaar, *The March to the Sea*, 93-94; and Emma Holmes, *The Diary of Miss Emma Holmes, 1861-1866*, ed. John F. Marszalek (Baton Rouge: Louisiana State University Press, 1979) 434.

vivals among the troops remained a feature of camp life until all the men had been finally dispersed to their homes. When the work of the Christian Commission delegates was finished, they counted themselves as singularly successful. John A. Cole, the top field agent for the Union armies in the eastern theater, described the last revivals with language reminiscent of the passage of Israel into the Promised Land.

> That pillar of fire which had ever gone before us, guiding in a way that we knew not, a way encompassed by difficulties and dangers, but made glorious by the favor of God, seemed now to rest upon every tabernacle and to shine upon every heart. Only a few short weeks did these scenes continue, the order came, the regiments passed away, each to its parent State, and henceforth the Army of the Potomac was to live only on the pages of history, and in the memories of men. And with it closed that work, . . . which had, in the name of Christ, brought healing to many a fainting body, and life to many a perishing soul.[30]

The best contemporary estimates of the total number of men converted in the Union forces in the Civil War placed that figure between 100,000 and 200,000—approximately five to ten percent of the total number of individuals actually in service during the conflict. Since this number includes only *conversions* and not the involvement of men who were either already Christians or interested spectators at the revivals, even it is an inadequate measurement of the fervor that swept through the Northern armies. So large a body of men had to be a conspicuous presence in the camps. The revivals, then, were probably the most vivid manifestation of what one historian has termed "the late, war-spawned elan" of the Union troops, and those religious gatherings contributed markedly to stimulating the confidence and enthusiasm that Northern soldiers possessed in the latter stages of the war.[31]

Throughout the wartime period, from the early gatherings at Washington in 1861 until the last grand encampment in 1865, revivals provided men in the Union armies with the encouragement they needed to continue the war effort. Although not every individual revival can be linked directly to a battlefield triumph of the North (revivals were always dependent on specific local conditions and the psychological readiness of the soldiers for them), revivalism on the whole was related to the overall

---

[30]Christian Commission, *Annual Report* 4 (1865): 107-108.

[31]Marvin R. Cain, "A 'Face of Battle' Needed: An Assessment of Motives and Men in Civil War Historiography," *Civil War History* 28 (1982): 24-26; Moorhead, *American Apocalypse*, 69-70; and J. G. Randall and David Herbert Donald, *The Civil War and Reconstruction*, 2nd ed., rev. (Lexington MA: D. C. Heath and Company, 1969) 530.

progress that the Union made in the war. The revivals gained force as the war's tempo accelerated and the soldiers felt themselves carried inexorably toward victory, and thus they tapped into the greater reservoir of emotions that the conflict inspired. Soldiers found themselves drawn daily into a close relationship not only with the church, but also with each other in the common experience of army life. Revivalism in the Union army, therefore, shaped profoundly the social environment in which the soldiers were engaged and made an invaluable contribution to the final victory of the North.

The Chariot of Fire: Religion, Revivalism, and Confederate Failure | 5

In *Four Years under Marse Robert,* his popular reminiscence about life in the Army of Northern Virginia, former Confederate officer Robert Stiles claimed that no account of the Southern military experience would be complete without reference to the religious life of the army. Stiles devoted a chapter to this subject, and in it he discussed some of his own work during a period of revivals. While visiting the graves of two soldiers in his artillery battery who had been killed in the battle of Chancellorsville, Stiles saw Allan, another member of his unit, kneeling at the graveside. Allan spoke to Stiles: " 'Bob, I am a mystery to myself. I don't see how I am to go up to the gun in to-morrow's fight and face temporal and eternal death.' " Stiles took that opportunity to talk about his religious faith, and when the conversation was over, Allan declared that Stiles had convinced him; he had accepted the lordship of Jesus Christ and knew that his sins had been forgiven. Deeply moved by what he heard, Stiles said that he had never before felt "such overpowering spiritual joy."

Two months passed after that incident; Stiles was sent to Richmond and did not return to the army until immediately after the Gettysburg campaign. When he came back to his old unit, he learned of Allan's death during the artillery duel on the last day at Gettysburg. As Allan was performing his duties beside his gun, an enemy shell had exploded nearby and left his body "gashed with wounds, the top of the skull blown off and the brain actually fallen out upon the ground in two bloody, palpitating lobes." Although Allan's comrades were sickened by this human wreckage, Stiles recognized that his death had in fact been a triumphant one. At the moment of his physical downfall and destruction, Allan had found the spir-

itual reward promised him when he was converted, and—as Stiles put it—
God's "chariot and horses of fire had caught him up into Heaven."[1]

Because of revivals during the war, thousands of Southerners like Stiles
and his friend believed that their sins had been forgiven and that by the
power of the Holy Spirit they had been given new identities within the
Christian fellowship. Described by some observers as the most religious
fighting unit ever, surpassing even the spiritual intensity of Cromwell's
Roundheads, the Confederate armies were estimated to have fostered the
conversion of at least 100,000 men. Massive revivals occurred on several
occasions throughout the conflict, and those who participated in them
testified to the effectiveness of those events in strengthening their faith
and the faith of their comrades. As was consistent with the claim of many
Southern churchmen that spiritual interest at home had noticeably declined, the growth of revivalism in the army seemed to indicate that the
religious focus for Southerners had indeed shifted.[2]

Revivals among the soldiers did not immediately begin in 1861, however. Like their counterparts in the Northern camps, many pious Confederates initially worried that army life was not conducive to their religious
improvement. Hugh White, a student at Union Theological Seminary in
Virginia, for example, had enthusiastically abandoned his studies and enlisted in the 4th Virginia Regiment. He soon become disheartened,
though, by the state of the army, and in his letters to his family he lamented the many privations that he felt forced to suffer: the failure of his
regiment to observe the Sabbath, the lack of regular preaching, and daily
association with profane and immoral men. Although a few soldiers in his
unit had expressed an interest in attending Bible readings and prayer
meetings, White confessed that the moral conduct of the Southern army
as a whole had only strengthened his evangelical belief in total human de-
pravity. Even his own Stonewall Brigade—reportedly the most pious of all

---

[1]Robert Stiles, *Four Years under Marse Robert* (New York: The Neale Publishing Company, 1903) 149-51.

[2]William W. Bennett, *A Narrative of the Great Revival Which Prevailed in the Southern
Armies During the Late Civil War Between the States of the Federal Union* (Philadelphia: Claxton, Remsen & Haffelfinger, 1877) 413; J. William Jones, *Christ in the Camp; or, Religion
in Lee's Army* (Richmond: B. F. Johnson & Co., 1887) 39, 317-19, 330-31, 338, 371-73,
390-91; J. William Jones, "The Morale of the Confederate Army," in *Confederate Military
History*, ed. Clement A. Evans (Atlanta: Confederate Publishing Company, 1899) 12:163
and Gorrell Clinton Prim, Jr., "Born Again in the Trenches: Revivalism in the Confederate Army" (Ph.D. diss., Florida State University, 1982) 55, 102-103, 137, 198-200.

the Southern forces—seemed to White to be too little concerned with religious matters.[3]

"I hear no sermons, hear none of the Songs of Zion, and am verily a stranger in a strange land," William Nugent complained to his wife concerning his experiences in the Confederate army. Indeed, at the same time he described his affliction with "the camp diarrhoea," Nugent declared that he suffered from a far worse "discomfort": "the want of the means of Grace." He found it virtually impossible to practice his faith in an environment that seemed to foster only evil behavior. Frank "Bull" Paxton, the adjutant of Stonewall Jackson's corps, also observed with regret that the majority of Southerners had actually "grown worse rather than better" on account of their military service. Although he thought that civilians were probably more greatly demoralized than the soldiers defending them, Paxton believed that army life had caused quite a few men to fall into unchristian habits. He knew that the war had made *him* more attentive to religion, but he feared that his reaction was not typical.[4]

Not until the war entered its second year did revivals become a distinct feature of life in the Southern camps. As late as October 1862, in fact, the Presbyterian Synod of Virginia lamented that no extensive religious activity had yet been apparent among the soldiers, and thus it officially resolved to take strenuous efforts to effect a revival in the army. Ironically enough, this synod was meeting at the same time that religious excitement began to emerge in units of the Army of Northern Virginia. An article in the Baptist *Religious Herald* noted that a revival was then in progress in General Roger Pryor's brigade and that 1,500 men had heard a preacher who had come from Richmond. The reporter for the *Herald* also described how several generals had changed military regulations in order to allow their men extra time to hear the preaching. Despite the waning of these revivals during the busy preparations for the Federal assault at Fredericksburg, they started again immediately after that battle. Beginning in William Barksdale's Mississippi brigade, the religious enthusiasm

---

[3]W. G. Bean, *The Liberty Hall Volunteers: Stonewall Jackson's College Boys* (Charlottesville: The University of Virginia Press, 1964) 11-12, 29-30, 127.

[4]William Lewis Nugent, *My Dear Nellie: The Civil War Letters of William L. Nugent to Eleanor Smith Nugent*, ed. William M. Cash and Lucy Somerville Howorth (Jackson: University Press of Mississippi, 1977) 113; and John Gallatin Paxton, ed., *The Civil War Letters of General Frank "Bull" Paxton, C. S. A.* (Hillsboro TX: Hill Jr. College Press, 1978) 79-80.

spread to fifteen brigades in Lee's army, and by the spring of 1863 it had affected roughly a third of the infantry brigades attached to that force.[5]

The letters of Dorsey Pender, a divisional commander under Lee, reveal the spiritual progress made by a pious soldier during the revivals held from the fall of 1862 to the spring of 1863. Pender wrote to his wife almost daily from the time he entered camp following the secession of North Carolina until his death after the battle of Gettysburg. He feared that his attention to Bible reading, praying, and churchgoing had been weak and that the distractions of military life at first had only increased his natural inclination to disregard religious duties. But in the face of the horrors he witnessed in the war, Pender became progressively more preoccupied with death and with the need for personal sanctity and faithfulness. As a result, he turned to the church, was baptized in the presence of his troops, and later was confirmed by the Episcopal bishop of Virginia. Pender's acceptance of the grace offered him in baptism, however, heightened his scrupulosity rather than alleviating it. He knew that "one can fall short of being a Christian, even when he appears to those of this world to be good"; he had to do all that he could and then trust in the mercy of Jesus.[6]

General Stephen D. Lee was another prominent soldier who was conscious of how he turned to religious interests at this time in the war. Although he was not baptized until 1868, Lee recounted how his experiences in battle had led him to give serious attention to religion. He dated his belief in God to the year 1862 and remembered that his first mature thoughts about religion occurred while gazing at the Union charge against his guns at Second Manassas. Robust men in good health at one moment were struck down and torn apart the next, and their bodies lay lifeless on the field in front of Lee. He thought then that the situation was absolutely ghastly, and it was horrifying to see even his enemies destroyed in this fashion. Lee concluded that "nothing but some unseen and superintending power" could tell him how all the carnage of the battle would end.[7]

---

[5]Bennett, *Narrative of the Great Revival,* 120, 204-208, 285; Jones, *Christ in the Camp,* 283, 293-97, 306-307, 337, 542; Synod of Virginia (Presbyterian), *Minutes* (1862): 310-15; *Religious Herald* 35 (1862): 51; *Southern Churchman* 28 (7 November 1862): 1; *Richmond Christian Advocate* 20 (9 October 1862): 2; ibid., 20 (26 February 1863): 1; ibid., 20 (12 March 1863): 1-2; and ibid., 20 (26 March 1863): 1.

[6]William Dorsey Pender, *The General to His Lady: The Civil War Letters of William Dorsey Pender to Fanny Pender,* ed. William W. Hassler (Chapel Hill: The University of North Carolina Press, 1965) 67-68, 71-76, 84, 95-96, 129, 135, 146, 181-82, 231.

[7]Herman Hattaway, *General Stephen D. Lee* (Jackson: University Press of Mississippi, 1976) 162.

In his history of the revivals in the Army of Northern Virginia, Baptist minister and former Confederate chaplain J. William Jones claimed that what he saw in the Southern camps was a "genuine and permanent work of grace" that produced results as lasting as any revival ever. Despite the hesitation of some who attributed the outbreak of revivalism only to "animal excitement" caused by the dangers of battle, Jones insisted that the intensity of religious interest in his army was the work of the Holy Spirit alone. The continual presence of death and the awesome threat of eternal damnation, of course, moved many soldiers to examine their consciences and make themselves aware of God's presence beside them. Although Jones and his fellow chaplains credited the physical dangers of army life with preparing soldiers psychologically for receiving the Gospel, they said that a man's decision to join the church was only a result of the divine will.[8]

Although the invasion of the North and the Gettysburg campaign in the summer of 1863 forced the cessation of regular prayer meetings, the beginning of more settled operations in August again renewed revivalistic activity in the army in Virginia. By the fall of 1863, what Southern churchmen later called the "Great Revival" was in full progress along the defensive line by the Rapidan and Rappahannock rivers. This revival lasted throughout the winter and into the spring of the next year before it was finally terminated by Grant's attacks in May 1864. According to reports from the army, approximately 7,000 men (or about ten percent of Lee's soldiers) were converted in that period, and at least 32 out of the 38 infantry brigades were touched by the revivals. Even in brigades that had shown little interest in religion during the first two years of the war, a religious interest gripped the soldiers.[9]

Many Confederates recorded detailed accounts of the revivals in Virginia during the fall and winter of 1863-1864. LeGrand Wilson of the 42nd Mississippi Regiment, for example, described the construction of a chapel by his brigade. This church offered protection from the weather when the

---

[8]Jones, *Christ in the Camp*, 391-95; and Jones, "Morale of the Confederate Army," 150-51, 164.

[9]Bennett, *Narrative of the Great Revival*, 263, 349; Jones, *Christ in the Camp*, 307, 319, 322-23, 347, 351, 390; Jones, "Morale of the Confederate Army," 151, 162-63; Prim, "Born Again in the Trenches," 106-107; J. F. J. Caldwell, *The History of a Brigade of South Carolinians, Known First as "Gregg's," and Subsequently as "McGowan's Brigade"* (Dayton OH: Morningside Bookshop, 1974) 112-23; John Hampden Chamberlayne, *Ham Chamberlayne—Virginian: Letters and Papers of an Artillery Officer in the War for Southern Independence, 1861-1865*, ed. C. G. Chamberlayne (Richmond: The Dietz Printing Co., Publishers, 1932) 183; and G. W. Nichols, *A Soldier's Story of His Regiment (61st Georgia)* (Kennesaw GA: Continental Book Company, 1961) 112, 125, 138-39.

whole unit gathered for services and served as a place of private worship for small groups of men who came there at every hour of the day and night. Wilson said that the chapel was always filled with worshipers, and for them it was "the very gate of Heaven." John Worsham of the 21st Virginia also wrote about an amphitheater that his brigade erected on the hillside near the camp. This amphitheater seated 2,000 people, and revivals were held there twice daily for several weeks in the fall of 1863. Worsham reported that

> the gathering each night of bronzed and grizzly warriors devoutly worshiping was a wonderful picture . . , and when some familiar hymn was given out those thousands of warriors would make the hill and dell ring.[10]

Revivalism among the Confederate forces in Virginia reached its peak in the summer of 1864, but by this time, the revivals had an unusual and critical effect on the performance of the troops in battle. George Cary Eggleston, whose *Rebel's Recollections* is an insightful account of his experiences as a soldier, claimed that "a sort of religious ecstasy took possession of the army" in the last year of the war. The behavior of some soldiers exceeded all reasonable human levels of bravery, as each man, convinced that "he was assisting at his own funeral," marched confidently forward to die for his country. Soldiers ceased to rely on their military leaders. They instead looked "for a miraculous interposition of supernatural power" on their behalf. The revivals functioned in this milieu as a symbolic cushion against defeat, for the disasters befalling Lee's army only strengthened the belief of religious soldiers that the South would receive victory through the will of God alone. Having accepted the spiritual support that the revivals offered them, men were led to surrender the hope that *they* could ever win the war by their own efforts. A cognizance of the ultimate futility of human aspirations pervaded the camp, and this attitude was to have an important impact on the Southerners' understanding of what was happening in the conflict.[11]

Revivals, sometimes as intense as those in Virginia, also took place in the Confederate Army of Tennessee. The first ones began in the winter of 1862-1863 and gained in strength as the year passed. In the summer,

---

[10]LeGrand James Wilson, *The Confederate Soldier*, ed. James W. Silver (Memphis: Memphis State University Press, 1973) 145-48; and John Worsham, *One of Jackson's Foot Cavalry*, ed. James I. Robertson, Jr. (Jackson TN: McCowat-Mercer Press, Inc., 1964) 113-14.

[11]George Cary Eggleston, *A Rebel's Recollections*, ed. David Donald (Bloomington: Indiana University Press, 1959) 177-79; and Bennett, *Narrative of the Great Revival*, 407.

furthermore, several prominent civilian ministers conducted a successful preaching mission in which they converted many soldiers—most notably Braxton Bragg, the army commander. Despite disruptions caused by the later movement of the army to the vicinity of Chattanooga, religious in-terest remained active, and only the withdrawal after the defeat at Mis-sionary Ridge brought a halt to the large-scale prayer meetings. During the Chickamauga-Chattanooga campaign, revivals were reported in at least eleven of the twenty-eight brigades of the Army of Tennessee, where "the largeness of the means of grace" (one observer reported) proved gratifying to the clergymen who worked among the troops. Consequently, the sol-diers in the western theater, like their counterparts in the East, partici-pated more and more enthusiastically in religious activities as the conflict swelled to its climax.[12]

The letters of James Street, a clergyman minister serving in the ranks of the 9th Texas Regiment, vividly reveal the excitement that gripped his army in the spring and summer of 1863. In April, Street noted that a Young Men's Christian Association, composed of fifty men of all denominations, had been formed in his brigade. He had heard that chaplains were at-tempting to organize a Y. M. C. A. in every brigade of the Army of Ten-nessee and was glad that they had finally undertaken serious evangelistic work. In early May, Street wrote to his wife that a spirit of revivalism had taken hold of most of the army. He had led prayer meetings in his regi-ment every night of the previous week and was impressed by what he thought was an unprecedented opportunity to labor as a minister. Street passionately hoped that the army revival would enable the Confederate people, chastened and purified by their wartime sufferings, to receive the favor of God. He knew that since only God could give military victory to one side or the other, a successful revival might assure the triumph of the South.[13]

The disaster at Missionary Ridge, however, had a far more profound impact on Confederate revivalism and morale than Street and others had foreseen. As the implications of the defeat at Chattanooga daily became clearer, Southern soldiers in the West seemed to shift the reliance that

---

[12]Bennett, *Narrative of the Great Revival*, 244, 280-81; Prim, "Born Again in the Trenches," 144-47; *The Religious Herald* 36 (14 August 1863): 2; and Emma Holmes, *The Diary of Miss Emma Holmes, 1861-1866*, ed. John F. Marszalek (Baton Rouge: Louisiana State University Press, 1979) 266.

[13]James Street to his wife, 9, 17 April, 8 May, 16 July, and 13 August 1863, in the James K. Street Papers, Southern Historical Collection, Library of the University of North Carolina at Chapel Hill.

they put on God—trusting him no longer as a giver of worldly success, but as a guarantor of spiritual victory instead. Joel Haley of the 37th Georgia, for instance, was discouraged to learn that the bravery his unit displayed at Chattanooga was insufficient to stay the Northern attack against its position. Haley turned to his faith to sustain his spirits. "The situation at present I do not profess to comprehend," Haley admitted. "I trust that *He* who doeth all things well, will deliver us in due time if we do our whole duty."[14]

The army spent the winter and spring of 1863-1864 at Dalton, Georgia, and there protracted prayer meetings and numerous conversions occurred in almost every brigade. "Nearly all our first Generals have joined the Church and the army is fast becoming . . . a God-fearing soldiery," one soldier triumphantly proclaimed. Religious interest peaked at Dalton, yet like the revivals in Virginia in 1864, those in Georgia were surrounded by an unusually pessimistic air. Indicative of this mood was a bizarre incident mentioned by several soldiers in their accounts of their wartime experiences. In the course of an evening prayer meeting in the 4th Tennessee Regiment, a nearby pine tree caught the sparks from a campfire illuminating the revival. The tree burst instantly into flame, burned through, crashed down upon the worshipers, and killed ten men. Although those who witnessed this scene later said that they rejoiced at the quick release of ten souls from their earthly cares, this event certainly must have filled observers with other, more equivocal, emotions and inspired in the survivors little confidence concerning the possible results of either their religious or military ventures. The revivals at Dalton, powerful and dramatic as they were, helped ready the Southern troops to look for an otherworldly triumph in the midst of more immediate defeats.[15]

After the Atlanta campaign, when military conditions were no longer favorable to widespread, organized work among the troops, revivalism in the Confederate armies of the West declined. However, the retreat and

---

[14]James Lee McDonough, *Chattanooga—A Death Grip on the Confederacy* (Knoxville: The University of Tennessee Press, 1984) 205.

[15]Nugent, *My Dear Nellie,* 180; Mark Perrin Lowrey, "An Autobiography," *Southern Historical Society Papers* 16 (1888) :376; Gross Alexander, *A History of the Methodist Church, South . . .* , vol. 11 of *American Church History Series* (New York: The Christian Literature Co., 1894) 72; Robert Manson Myers, ed., *The Children of Pride: A True Story of Georgia and the Civil War* (New Haven: Yale University Press, 1972) 1142; Sam R. Watkins, "Co. Aytch," *Maury Grays, First Tennessee Regiment; or, A Side Show of the Big Show,* ed. Bell Irvin Wiley (Jackson TN: McCowat-Mercer Press, Inc., 1952) 136; and James Cooper Nisbet, *4 Years on the Firing Line,* ed. Bell Irvin Wiley (Jackson TN: McCowat-Mercer Press, Inc., 1963) 175.

steady defeats in Georgia and the Carolinas in 1864 and 1865 still proved to be effective stimuli to the religious emotions of Southern soldiers. Steeled by the Dalton revivals to accept disappointments and to bear patiently the hardships of the war, Confederates waited with resignation for the final outcome of the military struggle. Henry Lay, Episcopal bishop of Arkansas and missionary in the army in Georgia, movingly depicted the baptism of General John Bell Hood in the fall of 1864. Amid the explosions of shells around them, Hood's soldiers watched as their leader was baptized; crippled by his wounds, Hood was "unable to kneel," but "supported himself on his crutch and staff, and with bowed head received the benediction." Hood's baptism symbolized the quest of Southern soldiers for the only support still available to them: the spiritual strength that their religious experiences provided.[16]

The situation in Virginia at this time was similar to that in the western theater. There had been an extended revival in the early months of 1864, but the difficulties of the spring and summer campaign hampered its continuation. So marked was the decline in the Army of Northern Virginia that, while almost eighty-five percent of the infantry brigades in Lee's army had been touched by revivals in the summer and fall of 1863, less than half the brigades were affected in 1864. By the fall of 1864, moreover, revivalism virtually came to an end, because the troops, numerically depleted and ever busy with maintaining the expanding defensive line at Petersburg, just had too little free time to participate in organized religious activities. As a result of the military misfortunes of the South, some observers feared that the army in Virginia was "dispirited" and that the men, seeing "nothing before them but certain death," had "fallen into a sort of hopelessness."[17]

In fact, the soldiers were still quite receptive to religious influences, but the clergymen who ministered to them no longer attempted to raise a general revival. They worked singly instead, preaching to small gatherings of men, praying with them, and distributing tracts even while the troops manned the Petersburg defenses. William Miller Owen of the Washington Artillery reported that "the whole army has taken to praying," a fact that gave him a slim but real sense of assurance. "If prayers accomplish anything," he thought, "we should whip this fight yet!" The prayers of

---

[16]Bennett, *Narrative of the Great Revival*, 401-402; Prim, "Born Again in the Trenches," 166-72; and *The Church Intelligencer* 5 (1864): 4.

[17]Prim, "Born Again in the Trenches," 124-27, 136-40; Bennett, *Narrative of the Great Revival*, 349, 362-63, 384; Jones, *Christ in the Camp*, 255-59, 353-63, 373-81; and Josiah Gorgas, *The Civil War Diary of General Josiah Gorgas*, ed. Frank E. Vandiver (Huntsville: The University of Alabama Press, 1947) 145.

Confederates like Owen, of course, were able to accomplish little to re-verse the course of the war. For most soldiers and chaplains left in the Southern army, the religious emphasis was then on the need of each man as an individual to prepare himself for the difficult days of defeat and hu-miliation ahead.[18]

How significant were these periodic outbreaks of religious fervor to the average soldier in the Southern camps? Historian Michael Barton pro-vides an answer in his *Goodmen*, a book in which he analyzed the char-acter and values of the Civil War soldiers. Barton discovered that more than three-quarters of the men in the sample he surveyed referred to re-ligion as an important factor in their lives—ranking it third on a list of fifteen significant "core values" on which soldiers in this period based their behavior. The individuals in his sample, furthermore, discussed a category that Barton labeled "moralism." Barton's research suggests, therefore, that spiritual and moral questions were a notable concern of those men who commented on their experiences in the army.[19]

Although Barton showed that religious beliefs and practices were im-portant to a majority of men from all regions and in all military ranks, he also indicated that there were some differences between the views of Northerners and Southerners on this subject. By and large, Confederate soldiers were more likely to mention religion, to profess a personal faith, and to express approval regarding the state of religious life in their army than Union soldiers were. This disparity between Southerners and North-erners was most apparent at the highest levels of the two armies, where many more Confederate generals than Union ones were known to have been regular churchgoers. Southern officers tended to express themselves freely about religion in a way that many Northern officers were not com-fortable doing. The generals (like U. S. Grant and William T. Sherman) who led the North to victory mainly involved themselves with military matters and evinced little interest in cultivating any spiritual sensitivity during the war.[20]

---

[18]William Miller Owen, *In Camp and Battle with the Washington Artillery of New Orleans* (Boston: Ticknor and Company, 1885) 361.

[19]Michael Barton, *Goodmen: The Character of Civil War Soldiers* (University Park: Pennsylvania State University Press, 1981) 24-33.

[20]Ibid., 25-33; and Bell Irvin Wiley, *The Life of Billy Yank: The Common Soldier of the Union* (Indianapolis: The Bobbs-Merrill Co., 1952) 358-59. For brief biographies of the Civil War generals, see Ezra J. Warner, *Generals in Gray: Lives of the Confederate Com-*

The most influential Christian soldiers were invariably acknowledged to be Southerners. Several Confederate corps commanders, such as Jeb Stuart, D. H. Hill, and John B. Gordon, were celebrated for their outstanding piety. Episcopal clergymen Leonidas Polk and William Nelson Pendleton exercised great authority and influence throughout the war. The three major army leaders in the western theater, Braxton Bragg, Joseph E. Johnston, and John Bell Hood, were all converted during the period of the army revivals. And, of course, Robert E. Lee and Stonewall Jackson of the Army of Northern Virginia were thought to epitomize the highest ideals of military valor and personal sanctity. Churchmen in both the North and the South praised these generals as exemplars of American piety.

Most Southerners unquestionably were pleased that their leading military figures were so religious. Yet this majority opinion was by no means universal throughout the South, and some who were associated with the army did voice reservations about the extreme piety of a few generals. Certainly Stonewall Jackson, for example, received a good deal of criticism (much of it after his death in 1863) for the peculiarities of his religious faith. His strict reliance on Providence was viewed as out of place even in the pious Army of Northern Virginia. George Cary Eggleston called Jackson's Calvinistic faith "little less than fatalism" and thought that the strictness of the general's life left him with an "utter lack of vivacity and humor." Richard Taylor, too, once a brigade leader under Jackson's command, believed that Jackson's soul was divided between two opposing forces: worldly, ruthless ambition at war with gentle Christian piety. Taylor portrayed Jackson's personality as a mixture of "genius" and "lunacy"; as a consequence, Jackson the soldier could never attain the spiritual peace that Jackson the Christian sought.[21]

The idea that religious fatalism marked the decision making of generals proved to be a troublesome one in the wartime South. Throughout the war, Southern evangelicals continually warned their countrymen to look beyond the events of the conflict and give their foremost attention to religious matters. Thomas R. R. Cobb, a brigadier general, won some dubious renown for his ability to interrupt patriotic gatherings and lecture his hearers about the primacy of their religious obligations. While trav-

---

manders (Baton Rouge: Louisiana State University Press, 1959) and Ezra J. Warner, *Generals in Blue: Lives of the Union Commanders* (Baton Rouge: Louisiana State University Press, 1964).

[21]Eggleston, *Rebel's Recollections*, 134; and Richard Taylor, *Destruction and Reconstruction: Personal Experiences of the Late War*, ed. Richard B. Harwell (New York: Longmans, Green and Co., 1955) 37, 89.

eling to the Confederate Congress in April 1861, Cobb and other digni-
taries spoke to crowds that congregated at train stations on the way. When
a group of onlookers called to him to speak on a Sunday afternoon, however, he delivered instead a stern address on the evils of Sabbath-break-
ing! "It was the only speech that was not cheered," he proudly recorded.
In December of the same year, Cobb reminded another audience that the
Confederacy could depend on neither its European nor its Northern sym-
pathizers to win independence; the only worthwhile assistance for which
the South could hope would come from God. In response to this address,
a number of prominent citizens expressed their fear that it might foster de-
featism, and they privately urged Cobb to adopt a less pessimistic tone. [22]

Mindful of the South's special need to win God's blessings, Christian
soldiers worried that their comrades should observe divine commandments and so be worthy of that providential favor. Ellison Capers, then
lieutenant-colonel of the 24th South Carolina (and later Episcopal bishop
of his state), wrote to his wife that the chronic intoxication of some generals might be an unforgivable affront to the Lord. He was deeply concerned about this misbehavior, because it imperiled the "sacred cause" for
which Southerners fought. General Edmund Kirby Smith believed that
God had spread confusion among the Northern hosts at the moment when
a victory at First Manassas seemed certain for them. This served as proof
to him that the Confederacy could not win the war merely by force of arms
but only through divine intervention on its behalf. He also was upset by
the heavy drinking in the army because it would arouse divine displeasure
and cause the downfall of the Confederate nation. And Josiah Gorgas, head
of the Confederate Ordnance Bureau and a convert to Episcopalianism in
the war, interpreted the losses at Gettysburg and Vicksburg as possible signs
of God's anger with the South. At the same time, Gorgas expressed anx-
iety that "the sins of the people of Charleston" and the "rottenness" of
that city would bring about its fall to the Union forces that were attacking
it. [23]

In March 1864, Jefferson Davis and fourteen of his generals were spot-
ted in St. Paul's Church in Richmond on a Sunday morning. Although
such a congregation may have inspired churchmen to hope that God would

---

[22]William B. McCash, *Thomas R. R. Cobb (1823-1862): The Making of a Southern Nationalist* (Macon GA: Mercer University Press, 1983) 242, 275.

[23]Ellison Capers to his wife, 2 August 1862, in the Ellison Capers Papers, Manuscript
Department, Duke University Library, Durham NC; Joseph Howard Parks, *General Edmund Kirby Smith, C. S. A.* (Baton Rouge: Louisiana State University Press, 1954) 136,
150; and Gorgas, *Civil War Diary*, 11, 50-51.

bless the designs of pious leaders, it also dismayed and upset other South-erners. Mary Chesnut said that a friend of hers, when seeing so many gen-erals in church, remarked on how "less piety and more drilling of commands would suit the times better." The same faith that helped religious soldiers seek a goal that transcended both the temporary elation of victory and the gloomy reality of defeat, after all, might only reconcile them prematurely to military failure. As Edmund Ruffin wrote in his diary, the "imbecility" displayed in the management of the Confederate war effort was directly attributable to "the morbid tenderness of conscience" of President Davis and leaders like him who had been converted during the conflict. Ruffin believed that the sensitivities that had led Davis to become "engaged in seeking to save his own soul" prevented him from giving appropriate at-tention to prosecuting the war against the enemies of the South.[24]

After the shock of the first major Confederate loss when Fort Donel-son surrendered in February 1862, Davis had reminded his countrymen that they could not expect to be exempt from "the rule of Divine govern-ment." God tested the faith of nations as well as individuals, Davis pro-claimed, by prescribing affliction as a "discipline" and a "chastening" that would lead people back to obedience to God's laws. In the first year of the war, at a time of generally high expectations, Southern evangelicals could still hope that military defeat did not mean that God did not favor them. Battlefield losses might only be a salutary purging of an otherwise healthy society. "God has blessed us even while we were undergoing Chastise-ment at his hands," William Nugent wrote to his wife from the army in Mississippi. Nugent knew that they might "suffer severely for a season," but he was still convinced (in May 1862) that "man's extremity is God's opportunity."[25]

As the war continued and the Confederacy suffered increasing hard-ships, however, the idea that the South was experiencing a wholesome discipline worried men like Ruffin who did not share the religious con-victions of the Southern leaders. And even these leaders themselves be-gan to wonder about the righteousness of their cause. When the summer of 1863 had passed, just as the "Great Revival" in the armies was starting,

[24]Mary Chesnut, Mary Chesnut's Civil War, ed. C. Vann Woodward (New Haven: Yale University Press, 1981) 585-86; John B. Jones, A Rebel War Clerk's Diary, ed. Earl Schenke Miers (New York: Sagamore Press, Inc., 1958) 349; and Edmund Ruffin, The Diary of Ed-mund Ruffin, ed. William Kauffman Scarborough (Baton Rouge: Louisiana State Univer-sity Press, 1972-1976) 2:459-60.

[25]Richard E. Beringer, et al., Why the South Lost the Civil War (Athens: The University of Georgia Press, 1986) 126; and Nugent, My Dear Nellie, 79.

statements about God's protection of the Confederate nation began to have a hollow sound. Robert E. Lee assured Davis that his "faith in the protection of an All Merciful Providence" had not yet been shaken. Davis for his part believed that "it [was] not for man to command success," but rather it was up to him to "strive to deserve it, and leave the rest" to God. Pious Southerners seemed to be attempting to quiet their religious fears by reassessing their positions and looking for promising signs in defeat itself.[26]

Throughout the diary he kept while he was confined at the prisoner-of-war camp at Johnson's Island in Lake Erie, Daniel R. Hundley, then a Confederate captain, pondered the meaning of his experiences as a prisoner. During the spring and summer of 1864, a series of revivals had swept through the ranks of the Southern prisoners, and Hundley himself had been active in them. These revivals helped him focus his thoughts about the relationship of the war to his religious faith. On 17 July 1864, a Southern officer who was a Methodist minister had preached in the open air to an assembly of about 2,000 men, and Hundley was deeply impressed by what he said. Although the trials that soldiers had suffered might have made some "querulous and both reckless and indifferent," Hundley saw that many Southern soldiers had learned a sense of Christian forbearance and submission instead. "Adversity has its lessons," he wrote,

> and those who will take the trouble patiently to master them will in the end be forced to acknowledge that it is oftentimes better to go up to the house of mourning than to the house of rejoicing. Bunyan wrote his *Pilgrim's Progress* inside the walls of a jail, and John Milton, grown old and blind, . . . gave to the world *Paradise Lost*. The enlightened Christian should learn to thank God for all the changes and vicissitudes of this mortal life, for the seeming evil as well as the good.[27]

For the great leaders of the Southern people like Davis, Lee, Johnston, and Hood, and for all the individual soldiers like Hundley and his many comrades touched by the army revivals, a belief in God's providence helped them endure the final months of agony before the Confederacy collapsed. By the end of the war, these Southerners were seeking a spiritual rather

---

[26]Beringer, et al., *Why the South Lost*, 266.

[27]Daniel R. Hundley, *Prison Echoes of the Great Rebellion* (New York: S. W. Green, 1874) 100-101. For other accounts of the revivals at Johnson's Island, see Edmund DeWitt Patterson, *Yankee Rebel: The Civil War Journal of Edmund DeWitt Patterson*, ed. John G. Barrett (Chapel Hill: The University of North Carolina Press, 1966) 158-61; 180-81; and John Washington Inzer, *The Diary of a Confederate Soldier: John Washington Inzer, 1834-1928*, ed. Mattie Lou Teague Crow (Huntsville AL: The Strode Publishers, Inc., 1977) 70, 94.

than a military victory, and they directed their emotional energies to that more transcendent goal. The cause was lost, the nation was dying, but the divine realm remained inviolate. Men who were devoutly Christian were forced to conclude that their defeat was consistent with the will of the sovereign God. In the revivals especially, a significant portion of the Southern troops gained solace and consolation as all chances for military success deserted them. Thus, having accepted the appropriateness of the losses they were suffering, they more easily surrendered their corporate de-sire to continue the war. Even before the Confederate armies formally ca-pitulated, Southerners accepted another kind of peace—the spiritual peace that God gave them.[28]

In the highest ranks of the Confederacy, public confessions of belief were common. Despite the painstaking attention that many Southern generals and common soldiers gave to spiritual matters, piety alone had not proved suffi-cient to bring the victory for which the army fought. And the results of the war certainly vindicated those who had urged their pious leaders to empha-size more forcefully than they did the need for human effort in prosecuting the conflict. Yet by 1865 moral victory looked better than no victory at all, and faith was some compensation for the failure of the military struggle. Re-ligious faith, honed by suffering in the wartime experience, remained as a symbol of the triumph that the South *had* won. In the eyes of many South-erners, then, churchgoers and nonchurchgoers alike, religion had become identified far more with failure than with success.

---

[28]Fred Hobson, *Tell About the South: The Southern Rage to Explain* (Baton Rouge: Lou-isiana State University Press, 1983) 80-81; and Beringer, et al., *Why the South Lost,* 334-35.

Defeat with God: The Postwar Perspective of the South | 6

At the end of the Civil War, as Southerners attempted to come to terms with their defeat, an atmosphere of profound discouragement pervaded the South. Fearing that the defeat of the Southern armies would be followed by the debasement of Southern culture as well, Richmond newspaper editor Edward Pollard immediately summoned his people to a new ideological battle with the North. The title of the book he wrote coined the phrase "Lost Cause," which became the byword for those who attempted to perpetuate the ideals of the Old South. The Confederacy, Pollard believed, had had heroes and memories that were worth celebrating; military losses had not destroyed the natural superiority of Southern society, but had merely dealt it a temporary setback. Following up on Pollard's work, Southern politicians, soldiers, poets, novelists, and journalists soon rallied to the defense of their region. They fought on all fronts against the incursion of Yankee ideas into the South and expressed the frustrations of Southerners about defeat, poverty, and social upheaval in their land.[1]

Religious ideology also proved to be an important element in the development of the Lost Cause and the myths about the Southern experience in the war. Connected to the process by which white Southerners recovered their self-esteem was the belief of churchgoers that the war had been a religious and moral crusade on the part of the Confederacy. "The South needs a book of 'Acts and Monuments' of Confederate martyrs,"

---

[1]Edward Pollard, *The Lost Cause* (New York: E. B. Treat & Co., 1866) 750-52; Thomas L. Connelly and Barbara L. Bellows, *God and General Longstreet: The Lost Cause and the Southern Mind* (Baton Rouge: Louisiana State University Press, 1982) 2-3; and Fred Hobson, *Tell About the South: The Southern Rage to Explain* (Baton Rouge: Louisiana State University Press, 1983) 88-89.

Robert Lewis Dabney wrote to his friend D. H. Hill in 1873. Aware of the value of polemical literature in molding public opinion on behalf of a cause, Dabney was convinced that a Southerner could compose a religious narrative as inspiring as Foxe's famous account of English Protestant martyrs. Churchmen like Dabney maintained the advocacy of Southern ideals for many years after the war and saw in the downfall of the Confederacy universal lessons about redemption in the midst of suffering. Eager to vindicate their people, churchmen sought to show how the South had actually emerged a *moral* victor with its honor intact, despite the momentary blemish of military defeat.[2]

Confederate defeat, of course, might have been interpreted differently than it was, since not all Southerners were as yet spiritually prepared for Appomattox. Faced with calamity, many Southern Christians often found themselves filled with despair. "I will try to be resigned," wrote one Southern woman. "I will try to look beyond the blindness of earthly passions, . . . but now, Oh God help me, it seems hard to bear." For some Southerners, the end of the war was reason enough to reject their religious faith altogether. They dismissed the explanation that defeat was one of the inscrutable actions of divine Providence and concluded instead that, if there were a merciful God, he would not have let the South suffer so terribly. And for others, the most plausible interpretation of failure was that their region had become estranged from God. To them, defeat appeared as a terrible and bloody testament of God's disfavor with an accursed people.[3]

It was probably impossible to expect that Southern churchmen could ever have acknowledged that slavery was a monumental error on their part and that *it* was the principal cause of God's seeming displeasure. Most white Southerners soon were reconciled to the end of slavery, and a few were even pleased to see it die, but virtually no one openly espoused the notion that slavery per se was sinful. The litany of guilt was far more general than that and included sins against which evangelicals had always railed: Sab-

---

[2]Robert Lewis Dabney to D. H. Hill, 1 December 1873, in the Daniel Harvey Hill Papers, Southern Historical Collection, Library of the University of North Carolina at Chapel Hill; and Charles Reagan Wilson, *Baptized in Blood: The Religion of the Lost Cause, 1865-1920* (Athens: University of Georgia Press, 1980) 7-8.

[3]Connelly, *God and General Longstreet*, 14-15; Dan T. Carter, *When the War Was Over: The Failure of Self-Reconstruction in the South, 1865-1867* (Baton Rouge: Louisiana State University Press, 1985) 90, 269; Daniel Aaron, *The Unwritten War: American Writers and the Civil War* (New York: Oxford University Press, 1975) 323; and Richard E. Beringer, et al., *Why the South Lost the Civil War* (Athens: The University of Georgia Press, 1986) 394.

bath-breaking, intemperance, political corruption, and the like. Because of these familiar transgressions, most Christians said, God had chosen to afflict the South with the war, and on them the final disaster of defeat was to be blamed. When slavery was advanced as a factor in the South's defeat, the institution itself was not condemned, but only its deficiencies and the inevitable abuses it had fostered. We have "strayed far and made void God's laws," one pious Southerner concluded, "and it was His own good pleasure to . . . chasten us and bring us back from the wicked paths in which we were recklessly wandering."[4]

Defeat, therefore, left the Southern churches with the burden of defending—all contrary evidence aside—the moral worthiness of their society, and long after the time when the Civil War should have been a dead issue, religious thinkers in the South were still obsessed with that subject. For Southerners, the war had become (in Robert Penn Warren's words) "the Great Alibi," the psychological heritage of a disastrous enterprise. Religious leaders were forced to turn backward and look to the past to find some inspiration to sustain them through a disconcerting and uncertain present. Southern Christians sensed that their moment of glory had already gone by and worried that the future offered them little chance for happiness. Only through nostalgic, romantic reminiscences of the Lost Cause and through stoic resignation were Southerners able to find some continuing meaning for their lives. Feeling desperately insecure and standing under apparent condemnation by both God and man, Southern churchmen soon began to argue that their suffering was not really a curse; it was actually a testament to their vindication in the court of divine justice.[5]

For many years after Appomattox, therefore, clergymen in the South spoke of the spiritual benefits adversity provided. Although temporal prosperity made men arrogant and seduced them into believing they did not need God, hardship taught forbearance and Christian humility. A passage in William Faulkner's novel The Unvanquished captures the poignant mood of the Southern churches at the conclusion of the war. Faulkner describes Brother Fortinbride, a lay preacher and former soldier, who, as the conflict drew to a close and defeat confronted the South, knew that there was no further chance that God would give victory to the Confederate armies. In the face of the gloom his people felt, Fortinbride coun-

---

[4]Carter, When the War Was Over, 92.

[5]Robert Penn Warren, The Legacy of the Civil War: Meditations on the Centennial (New York: Random House, 1961) 54.

seled them to turn their attention away from the world and toward religious truths instead. He contrasted an unfaithful North, mad in its carnal delight at winning the war, with a chastened South, a region forced to its knees by misery. Fortinbride concluded that there was an important spiritual lesson in the recent history of the South: "victory without God is mockery and delusion, but . . . defeat with God is not defeat" at all. This theme of religious victory in the midst of temporal defeat—the sole hope in a demoralized time—provided a seductive figure of strength for the downcast South.[6]

A real clergyman drew much the same lesson as Fortinbride in his own reflections on the collapse of the Confederate nation. Writing to a friend after a recent meeting of the Episcopal Church in Virginia, Joshua Peterkin wondered whether a Southern victory in the war would really have been a worthwhile accomplishment after all. The Confederate soldiers, he wrote, had "indeed done wonders, but had they been successful, the fruits of their labours would, in all probability, have been reaped by a set of heartless politicians." Peterkin compared the South to the biblical Job, whose moral and spiritual worth was tested and fully revealed only when he suffered afflictions. Instead of falling prey to arrogance, which so often follows in the wake of temporal prosperity, Southerners were going to learn Christian humility. "It is better to endure adversity," Peterkin sadly surmised.[7]

Abram Joseph Ryan, a Roman Catholic priest and former army chaplain, wrote prolifically on these themes, and in his poems he repeatedly described how the South had been "consecrated" by its sorrows. Known as the "Poet Priest of the Lost Cause," Ryan depicted the melancholy condition of the Southern states, "barren, beautiless, and bleak," filled with ruins from the war. While the mighty North might enjoy a brief moment of triumph, in the course of time its victory would be forgotten. "Calvaries and crucifixions take the deepest hold of humanity," Ryan wrote, and "the sufferings of the right are graven deepest on the chronicle of nations." Although "crowns of roses" worn by conquerors had always faded, only "crowns of thorns" inflicted upon the conquered have endured. In Ryan's estimation, the debasement of the South symbolized God's enduring love for the Southern people:

---

[6]William Faulkner, *The Unvanquished* (New York: Vintage Books, 1966) 154-55.

[7]Joshua Peterkin to William Nelson Pendleton, from Richmond, 28 September 1865, in the William Nelson Pendleton Papers, Southern Historical Collection, Library of the University of North Carolina at Chapel Hill.

> *Yes, give me the land*
> *That is blest by the dust,*
> *And bright with the deeds,*
> *Of the down-trodden just.*
>
> • • •
>
> *Yes, give me the land*
> *Of the wreck and the tomb;*
> *There's grandeur in graves—*
> *There's glory in gloom.*
> *For out of the gloom*
> *Future brightness is born;*
> *As, after the night*
> *Looms the sunrise of morn.*[8]

William Nelson Pendleton, once chief of artillery of the Army of Northern Virginia and later rector of the Episcopal parish in Lexington, Virginia, where Robert E. Lee was a vestryman, was another clergyman who linked the Southern experience to that of the crucified Christ. Arrested immediately after the war for his refusal to reinstate the prayer for the President of the United States in the worship services of his church, Pendleton strenuously resisted the Northern occupation of the South. He contended that Southerners had become a captive people who were "related towards the government and Northern people somewhat as were our Blessed Lord and the Apostles towards the Roman authorities." Believing that Southerners lived under foreign domination and suffered persecution comparable to that borne by first-century Christians, Pendleton never made peace with the North. Instead, his rhetoric was filled with his anguished feelings, and he imagined that his countrymen were forced to endure martyrdom at the hands of the occupying Northerners.[9]

"Saint Paul's Vision of Victory," an article in the 1866 *Southern Presbyterian Review,* used the experience of the South as a parable for the suffering of the just. In this piece, Jonathan Bocock tried to find a theological meaning in the history of the war. Although the sorrows of the Southern

---

[8]Abram Joseph Ryan, *Poems: Patriotic, Religious, Miscellaneous* (Baltimore: John B. Piet, 1880) 27-28, 98-99, 137, 140, 273-75; Walter Burgwyn Jones, ed., *Confederate War Poems* (Nashville: Bill Coats, Ltd., 1984) 58; and Wilson, *Baptized in Blood,* 58-59.

[9]Thomas L. Connelly, *The Marble Man: Robert E. Lee and His Image in American Society* (Baton Rouge: Louisiana State University Press, 1977) 37-39; and Wilson, *Baptized in Blood,* 63.

people might seem unendurable, Bocock reminded his readers that "all things work together for good" for those who love God and that they could have confidence that God would ultimately accomplish what was best for his "chosen people." Just as God had raised Jesus from the dead and restored him to glory after his worldly defeat, so he would save those who followed him faithfully through whatever ignominy the wicked forced upon them. Although in the eyes of the world the righteous appeared to have been defeated, their ultimate vindication was certain. [10]

The South's wartime experience, then, taught many Southerners how illusory worldly ambitions were. Consistent with the tendency of Southern religion to deemphasize the value of secular involvement, the South's defeat confirmed that justification was best sought outside this world. By admitting their earthly failure, however, spokesmen for the Southern churches were able to shift the focus for the superiority of their region and thus could remain confident of their own rectitude. The prayerful Southern people, they said, had turned the other cheek to their conquerors and had accepted that Northerners were more adept in temporal matters. Like witnesses to the fact that Christian truth often stands condemned by evil men in the present age, these churchmen dared tell the successful North that success was not really all that important, and they asked Northerners to appreciate instead the virtues of failure. Employed in this way, the religious elements within the myth of the Lost Cause strengthened Southern self-identity and enabled religion to emerge as a potent force uniting the postwar society of the South.

The Confederate army itself was an important symbol of the moral victory the South had won. Central to the argument about the righteousness of their region was the Southerners' belief that the army had kept the faith of their men alive throughout the many trials of the war. Carlton McCarthy of the Richmond Howitzers, for example, wrote that Christianity, stripped of all its "sensual allurements" in the camp, took a powerful hold on the Southern soldiers. The pious soldier read in the Bible the orders of "the Captain of his salvation" and gave Jesus Christ the same attention he gave his earthly commander when his unit formed for battle. Robert Stiles thought that the elevating characteristics of army service explained why the New Testament used military imagery more than any other as a metaphor for the Christian life. As Stiles noted, "when the Son of

---

[10]Jonathan Bocock, "Saint Paul's Vision of Victory," *Southern Presbyterian Review* 16 (1866): 326-27; 332-33, passim.

God 'marveled' at a Roman soldier's *faith*, . . . the man himself traced this faith to the teachings of his military life," for he had "learned *as a soldier* the two great lessons of subjection and supremacy, of obedience and command." And as another writer expressed it, religious interest among the Southern soldiers had been so strong that it transformed the army into a veritable "sacramental host."[11]

The faith and military brilliance of some of the leading Confederate generals were employed as primary evidence that demonstrated the moral purity of the Southern cause—no soldier being more admired than Stonewall Jackson. In response to the tremendous grief that accompanied Jackson's untimely death, his mentor, Robert Lewis Dabney, published the initial hagiographic biography of the general. In the pamphlet *True Courage*, Dabney argued that Jackson's Christian belief was the single most important aspect of his character; because of his faith, Jackson feared nothing and achieved victories in the face of terrible perils. Like "Moses . . . upon the Mount of God," Jackson engaged in prayer before every battle, and his piety and that of his men brought victories from Manassas to Chancellorsville. Commissioned by the Jackson family to write a full-scale biography as well, after the war Dabney continued to gather details about his former leader. His 1866 work, *Life and Campaigns of Lieut.-Gen. Thomas J. Jackson*, was lengthy and exhaustive, covering both Jackson's military exploits and his religious character. In this book, Dabney demonstrated to Southern believers that Jackson was unsurpassed in both military skill and Christian piety.[12]

John Esten Cooke, famous in the postwar era for the publication of many romantic sagas about the Confederate army, released the first book-length biography of Jackson in 1863. This reappeared in a revised and expanded edition in 1866 as *Stonewall Jackson: A Military Biography*. Cooke said that Jackson was "a true 'soldier of the Cross,'" who in battle relied not on the mere strength of arms, but on God's overruling Providence. Recalling images from the English Civil War, Cooke portrayed his subject as having "the very bull-

---

[11]Carlton McCarthy, *Detailed Minutiae of Soldier Life in the Army of Northern Virginia, 1861-1865* (Richmond: B. F. Johnson Publishing Co., 1899) 215-17; Robert Stiles, *Four Years under Marse Robert* (New York: The Neale Publishing Co., 1903) 367-68; and William W. Bennett, *A Narrative of the Great Revival Which Prevailed in the Southern Armies During the Late Civil War Between the States of the Federal Union* (Philadelphia: Claxton, Remsen & Haffelfinger, 1877) 275.

[12]Robert Lewis Dabney, *True Courage: A Discourse Commemorative of Lieut. General Thomas J. Jackson* (Richmond: Presbyterian Committee of Publication, 1863) 8-9, 14-16, 22; and Robert Lewis Dabney, *Life and Campaigns of Lieut.-Gen. Thomas J. Jackson* (New York: Blelock & Co., 1866) passim.

Stonewall Jackson, the principal figure in the "pantheon" of Confederate religious heroes (Mary Anna Jackson, *Memoirs of Stonewall Jackson by His Widow* [Louisville: The Prentice Press, 1895] 480-91).

dog pertinacity and iron nerve of Cromwell." "Few human beings ever equalled [Jackson] in the great art of making war," Cooke wrote, and "fewer still in purity of heart and life." He was a stern prophet-warrior—a hybrid of an Old Testament Joshua and a Cromwell—stubbornly invoking the direction of his forces from the "God of Battles."[13]

During its short publishing life, The Land We Love, a journal established in 1866 to advance Southern literature, history, and agriculture, became one of the principal organs of the Lost Cause. Edited by D. H. Hill, a prominent Presbyterian layman and Confederate general, this magazine frequently contained articles about the religious life of the Southern armies and linked the supposed superiority of the South to the piety of its fighting men. In the 1867 edition, for instance, T. W. Hall composed a piece that recounted the religious experiences of soldiers in the Army of Tennessee. The evangelization of the soldiers in camp and the revival spirit that gripped his army, Hall believed, were essential elements in the history of the Civil War. In 1868, The Land We Love contained two articles by Gabriel Manigault entitled "The Decay of Religion in the South." Although this title might suggest that Manigault despaired of the religious condition of his region, the opposite was actually true. His articles described how newly liberated blacks were subverting the otherwise high tone of the South and thereby debasing the "cause" to which white Christians had given so much support. Responding to a decadent present, Manigault lauded martyred generals like Jackson and Leonidas Polk, who in the war had defended not only the political rights of the South, but also the "religious truth" for which the Confederacy had stood.[14]

Other writers soon elaborated on these themes that men like Dabney, Cooke, and Hill originally made prominent. The first book that chronicled the religious life of the Confederate forces in its entirety appeared in 1877. In A Narrative of the Great Revival Which Prevailed in the Southern Armies, William W. Bennett argued that Southerners should take heart from the experience of camp life in their armies. Bennett, who during the

---

[13]John Esten Cooke, Stonewall Jackson and the Old Stonewall Brigade, ed. Richard B. Harwell (Charlottesville: University of Virginia Press, 1954) 9, 11, 32-33, 42; John Esten Cooke, Stonewall Jackson: A Military Biography (New York: D. Appleton and Company, 1866) 464; and Mary Jo Bratton, "John Esten Cooke and His 'Confederate Lies,' " The Southern Literary Journal 13 (1981): 76-77.

[14]T. W. Hall, "Religion in the Army of Tennessee," The Land We Love 4 (1867): 127-31; Gabriel Manigault, "The Decay of Religion in the South," The Land We Love 5 (1868): 202-203, 300-301; and Ray M. Atchison, "The Land We Love: A Southern Post-Bellum Magazine of Agriculture, Literature, and Military History," North Carolina Historical Review 37 (1960): 506.

war had headed the Soldiers' Tract Association of the Methodist Episcopal Church, South, actively promoted the image of the Confederate army
as a religious force. He believed that the Southern army camp had been
"a school of Christ" and that the "moral miracles" that had occurred there
were the greatest of all history and a " 'silver lining' to the dark and heavy
cloud" of the war. Writing at the end of the Reconstruction period, moreover, Bennett appealed straightforwardly to Northerners and asked them
to accept the truth of his narrative. The army revivals, he claimed, had
helped ready the South to accept defeat and prepared Southerners to live
at peace with their former enemies. Since the soldiers' religious faith had
enabled them to endure defeat with equanimity, Bennett knew that their
piety would also bring lasting harmony to the reunited nation.[15]

Published a decade after Bennett's book, *Christ in the Camp; or, Religion in Lee's Army* by J. William Jones proved to have an even more profound influence on American religion. First released serially in the Baptist
Religious Herald this work provoked a flurry of confirmatory letters to the
editor in support of Jones's theories about the relationship of Southern piety
and Confederate army service. Compiled from published materials, from
the correspondence and reminiscences of ministers in the Confederate
ranks, and from Jones's own autobiographical accounts of his service as a
chaplain, *Christ in the Camp* demonstrated that soldiers in the Army of
Northern Virginia were religious as well as military heroes. As much a collection of universal lessons about morality as an actual history of religious
life in Lee's army, this book was upbeat and beguiling, and Jones directed
it to readers in both sections of the country. Like Bennett, Jones concen-
trated on describing how the postwar strength of the Southern churches
derived from the spiritual invigoration that men had received during their
army service.[16]

For example, Jones discussed a soldier whom he had baptized in the army
and then met again after the war. That man had been raised in an affluent
family and had prepared for a professional career, but when the war began,
he laid aside his personal ambitions and offered himself as a soldier. In the
course of the conflict, his property was destroyed, his money was dissipated,
and he was maimed by the loss of his right arm in battle. When Jones en-
countered him many years later, he was working as a farmer, trying to eke

---

[15]Bennett, *Narrative of the Great Revival*, 16, 73, 230, 426-27.

[16]J. William Jones, *Christ in the Camp; or, Religion in Lee's Army* (Richmond: B. F.
Johnson & Co., 1887) passim; Wilson, *Baptized in Blood*, 43-44; and Rufus B. Spain, *At
Ease in Zion: A Social History of Southern Baptists, 1865-1900* (Nashville: Vanderbilt Uni-
versity Press, 1967) 27.

out a meager living from the land that was left him. Although Jones at first saw the ex-soldier as an object for his pity, the man would not accept it; instead he replied, " 'Oh, Brother Jones, that is all right. *I thank God that I have one arm left and an opportunity to use it for the support of those I love.*' " Jones believed that this soldier's attitude exemplified all the best effects of the religious conversions that took place during the army revivals. These converts looked beyond the misfortunes the South had suffered and industriously set themselves to work rebuilding their lives.[17]

Jones was secretary of the Southern Historical Society from 1873 to 1887. Throughout that period, he literally controlled the shape of the Lost Cause through the publication of documents relating to the Confederacy in volumes of the *Southern Historical Society Papers*. He participated in the activities of many Confederate veterans' groups and was also chaplain at the University of Virginia and later at the University of North Carolina—being active, thus, at the heart of both the intellectual and popular culture of the South. Jones also continued to write about the virtues of the soldiers he had known in the war. He composed a highly significant article entitled "The Morale of the Confederate Army" for the multivolume *Confederate Military History*. Clement Evans, the editor of that series, was a former brigadier who had been converted during his army service and had entered the Methodist ministry in 1866. Since he wanted a man with experience similar to his own to write about what he regarded as a crucial topic in his series, Evans specifically sought out Jones to work on that task. In this article, Jones argued that the high morale of the Southern armies was a result of their containing so many brave, self-sacrificing Christians, men who willingly laid down their lives for the promise of a heavenly reward.[18]

In writing about the life and military career of Robert E. Lee, Jones reached the height of his influence as an evangelist of the Lost Cause. Serving as pastor of the Baptist church in Lexington at the time of Lee's death in 1870, Jones was given material by the Lee family for use in a proposed memorial volume about the general. Published in 1875, this book, *Personal Reminiscences, Anecdotes, and Letters of Gen. Robert E. Lee,* characterized with reverential epithets not only Lee the man, but also the highest ideals of the cause for which he stood: "Duty," "Modest Humility, Simplicity, and Gentleness," a "Spirit of Self-Denial," and a "Christian Character." Jones believed that his former commander was the greatest

---

[17]Jones, *Christ in the Camp,* 464.

[18]J. William Jones, "The Morale of the Confederate Army," in *Confederate Military History*, ed. Clement A. Evans (Atlanta: Confederate Publishing Co., 1899) 12:148, 175, 186, 193; Wilson, *Baptized in Blood,* 119-22, 130; and Connelly, *Marble Man,* 41-42.

soldier *and* the most faithful Christian whom America had ever known. In another book, published in 1906 near the end of his life, Jones emphasized again his ideas about Lee's strong religious faith. The final chapter of Jones's *Life and Letters of Robert Edward Lee* was devoted to a lengthy analysis of Lee's piety and its role in the development of his saintly character. Lee's support of worship and Sabbath observance had brought the Southern soldiers continually under the influences of Christian preaching, and his own personal piety had had an inestimable effect on the moral tone of the Army of Northern Virginia.[19]

Jones's image of Lee, the conscientious and religious soldier, represented in many ways a perfect expression of the ideals of popular evangelicalism in America. Faithful to stereotypes of American religion, Jones minimized the formal aspects of religion in the Confederate camp and emphasized instead its spontaneous, unaffected features. In his *Personal Reminiscences*, Jones recounted an incident among the Southern forces in November 1863. On the night before a battle, Lee happened upon some soldiers in prayer, joined them, and let them give him spiritual counsel regarding his actions in the campaign ahead. An engraving in the book (later reprinted in Bennett's *Narrative of the Great Revival*) illustrated that scene as Jones remembered it: Lee and the other officers standing with their heads bowed, and the private soldiers kneeling beside them, as they all offered prayers for themselves and for their cause. Significantly, the participation of clergy or chaplains was given little regard, and instead the prayers of laymen, Lee the paladin and his pious comrades in arms, received the special attention. Lee's spiritual leadership, it seemed, resulted not from any ecclesiastical standing that he possessed, but simply from his outstanding personal sanctity. Jones's depiction of religion in the Confederate army, consequently—a place where faith was democratic, nonhierarchical, and nonclerical—was actually a fitting description of American evangelicalism itself.[20]

In the myth of the Lost Cause, Lee represented the spiritual triumph of the South amid the cruelties of defeat, and he became a major figure in the writings of Southern churchmen in the postwar era. His life, in fact, provided a perfect answer to the troubling theological question that Southerners asked themselves—namely, why was the righteous South defeated by the supposedly godless North? Lee was a symbolic Christ figure,

---

[19]J. William Jones, *Personal Reminiscences, Anecdotes, and Letters of Gen. Robert E. Lee* (New York: D. Appleton, 1875) xi-xiv, 445; and J. William Jones, *Life and Letters of Robert Edward Lee, Soldier and Man* (New York: The Neale Publishing Company, 1906) 467.

[20]Jones, *Personal Reminiscences*, 417.

morally spotless, betrayed by the sins of lesser men, and forgiving of those who overpowered him. His example was continually advanced as the classic case of the good man who suffered and was defeated, but whose character was honed to perfection by pain. Molded into an appealing image of the gentle yet heroic Jesus, Lee's Confederate career shone like a beacon of rectitude in the midst of degradation and ruin.[21]

Randolph Harrison McKim, an Episcopal minister and former staff officer and chaplain in the Army of Northern Virginia, also emerged as an important interpreter of Lee's religious significance in the postbellum South. In a sermon preached shortly after Lee died, McKim extolled him as a paragon of military, civic, and religious virtues, the archetype of the Christian man. Despite the hardship of the downfall of the Confederacy and the temptation to become bitter as a result, Lee's spirit was never conquered. By his attention to spiritual rather than temporal values, McKim said, Lee lived a life characterized by moral triumph. As McKim's eulogy

The Southerners' romantic view of the piety of Robert E. Lee and his men (Bennett, *Narrative of the Great Revival*, 205).

---

[21]Connelly, *Marble Man*, 94-95; Wilson, *Baptized in Blood*, 48-49; and Connelly, *God and General Longstreet*, 29.

of Lee made plain, the South had indeed brought victory out of defeat and had transformed the shame of its worldly failure into a glorious, metaphysical triumph. [22]

McKim continued as a clerical spokesman for Lee's virtues long after 1870. As rector of the Church of the Epiphany in Washington, D.C. at the end of the century, he occupied an especially strategic position from which to influence the thought of American churchgoers in every section of the country. McKim called on all citizens to recognize that the motives of the South in the Civil War had been just as "high and as pure" as those of the North. Because Lee, "that . . . stainless hero," had taught his men to accept their defeat with grace and forgiveness, the South was vindicated, McKim asserted, in spite of its losses on the battlefield. Lee possessed a truly "Christ-like spirit of self-sacrifice," giving up the success he would have enjoyed as a Union general to protect those he loved in his homestate of Virginia. Thus, in peace as well as in war, Lee bore in noble fashion the burdens of his people. [23]

Southern ministers worked hard to publicize the saintly character of commanders like Jackson and Lee, and thereby they placed religion at the heart of the mythology about the Civil War. At the same time, pious ex-generals such as Clement Evans and John B. Gordon (first commander of the United Confederate Veterans) held key posts in groups that were formulating the ideology of the Lost Cause. Churches throughout the South, they said, were filled with men who dated their religious awakenings to the army revivals during the war and had returned home with a determination to continue as faithful Christians. In his influential *Reminiscences* about his wartime experiences, Gordon praised the faith of his soldiers and described how it had enabled them to recover from their losses in the conflict. The religion of the typical Southern soldier, Gordon noted, was not one "of hate, of vindictiveness, of debauchery" that promised heavenly fulfillment only to those who died in battle. Instead, it was deep and intense, and banished "all unworthy passions" from the heart. The religious convictions of Southern men were made stronger by both their army ex-

---

[22]Randolph Harrison McKim, *In Memoriam: Good Men a Nation's Strength* (Baltimore: John Murphy & Co., 1870) passim.

[23]Randolph Harrison McKim, *The Motives and Aims of the Soldiers of the South in the Civil War* (Nashville: United Confederate Veterans, 1904) 3, 28, 32, 34; Randolph Harrison McKim, *The Soul of Lee* (New York: Longmans, Green and Co., 1918) 202-203, 207, 210-11; and Wilson, *Baptized in Blood*, 49.

periences and defeat, and these convictions had prepared them to face the trials of the Reconstruction period with a positive, hopeful attitude.[24]

William Porcher DuBose, a Confederate officer ordained to the Episcopal ministry near the end of the war and later a prominent theologian, poignantly summed up the profound effect that his military service had had upon his religious development. In his autobiography, he described the point when he admitted to himself that the Confederate cause was hopeless. He was in camp after darkness had fallen, and in this setting he felt despondent and absolutely alone. Yet at the very moment of this, his deepest depression, DuBose felt the presence of God beside him. "Without home or country, or any earthly interest or object before me," he wrote, "I redevoted myself wholly and only to God, and to the work and life of His Kingdom." DuBose believed that what had happened to him in the war was responsible for his conversion, and it had forced him to realize for the first time how only divine, eternal truths were secure amid the misfortunes of life. With the collapse of the Confederacy and the subsequent decline of Southern civilization, the church remained the single institution capable of maintaining the ideals for which the South once had stood.[25]

After the war, spokesmen for the Lost Cause pointed with special pride to the tenacity of their people's religious faith. Although the South had lost on the battlefield, Southerners rejoiced that their men still retained the simple piety of a bygone day. Romantic images of gallant, outnumbered soldiers praying with their generals around the campfire gave the Lost Cause an undeniably appealing and inspiring quality. Religious apologists for the South needed no better justification than this to argue on behalf of the enduring moral strength of the defeated Confederacy. Honor, they learned, could still be won without attaining any of the other war aims of the South. Indeed, honor apparently was best won *without* military victory at all. Defeat in the Civil War and the preoccupation of Southerners with the past, rather than forcing the collapse of the religious tradition of the South, actually helped rejuvenate it. As Southern evangelicals had always told their countrymen, spiritual, not temporal, goals were the only ones really worth pursuing.

----

[24]John B. Gordon, *Reminiscences of the Civil War* (New York: Charles Scribner's Sons, 1903) 233-34.

[25]William Porcher DuBose, *Turning Points in My Life* (New York: Longmans, Green and Co., 1912) 49-50.

EPILOGUE
Religion and National Reconciliation

During the last quarter of the nineteenth century, belligerency between the North and South diminished, and many Americans seemed eager to forget much of the enmity that had once divided the two sections. As early as 1867, a poem entitled "The Blue and the Gray" gave voice to these sentiments. The poem described the reunion of Northern and Southern soldiers in heaven and the mystical bonds that existed among earthly mourners in common sorrow for their sons who died in the war.

> From the silence of sorrowful hours
>   The desolate mourners go,
> Lovingly laden with flowers,
>   Alike for the friend and the foe:—
>   Under the sod and the dew,
>   Waiting the judgment day;
>   Under the one, the Blue
>   Under the other, the Gray.
>
> • • • • • • •
>
> No more shall the war-cry sever,
>   Or the winding rivers be red.
> They banish our anger forever
>   When they laurel the graves of the dead:—
>   Under the sod and the dew,
>   Waiting the judgment day;
>   Love and tears for the Blue
>   Tears and love for the Gray.

Such hopeful and sentimental themes of fellowship soon appeared in popular literature and indicated a broad-based desire to honor the heroism of *all* the soldiers. Old hatreds gradually dissolved into nostalgic recollections of the late war, and reconciliation became a common political, literary, and religious motif.[1]

Several important factors, of course, pressed Northerners and Southerners toward reconciliation. Northern business interests favored a course of moderation, since a rapid and effective recovery of the South benefited those who had invested capital there. In the political sphere, the Democratic party was eager to forget the conflict and reestablish its dominance as the one truly national party. Republicans, on the other hand, learned in 1876 that leniency towards the South could be advantageous to their control of the presidency. As the crusading zeal of erstwhile reformers faded, virtually all white Americans wished to see the race issue die, and they were content to let white Southerners deal with blacks in any way they chose. And in the literary world, the Old South emerged as a desirable subject by the end of the century. Fictional portrayals of Southern blacks—religious yet superstitious, penniless yet happy, and childishly dependent on whites—helped placate the feelings of any Northern readers who felt guilty about leaving the South on its own again. The disparaging remark of Albion Tourgee, the former carpetbagger, was apt: American literature had become "not only Southern in type but distinctly Confederate in sympathy."[2]

This process by which Americans were eventually reunited after the terrible four-year struggle proved, naturally enough, to be a complex and tortuous one. Many Northerners were at first anxious to prosecute the peace as vigorously as they had prosecuted the war, and they wanted to garner the fruits of a victory that had cost them so much in terms of lives and dollars. The Republican party had been born in strife over issues that won it support only in the North, and its leaders assumed that keeping the sectional dispute alive would be the best means of maintaining Republican political strength. In the churches, too, clergy of both sections refused to

---

[1]Paul H. Buck, *The Road to Reunion, 1865-1900* (Boston: Little, Brown and Company, 1947) passim; and Sydney E. Ahlstrom, *A Religious History of the American People* (New Haven: Yale University Press, 1972) 688-89.

[2]Robert A. Lively, *Fiction Fights the Civil War: An Unfinished Chapter in the Literary History of the American People* (Chapel Hill: The University of North Carolina Press, 1957) 21-23; Anne Rowe, *The Enchanted Country: Northern Writers in the South, 1865-1910* (Baton Rouge: Louisiana State University Press, 1978) xvii-xix; and Buck, *Road to Reunion*, passim.

forgive the foes against whom their people had fought. The results of the war confirmed the Northerners' sense of their own righteousness, and they chastised Southern churchmen for perpetrating a double sin: first, supporting the evil institution of slavery, and then plunging the nation into war in a vain attempt to keep their slaves in bondage. Northerners prayed that on Judgment Day their enemies would be—in the words of Henry Ward Beecher—"whirled aloft and plunged downward forever and forever in endless retribution." A righteous God, Beecher and his colleagues declared, could never grant forgiveness to the "guiltiest and most remorseless traitors" who had caused "this ocean of blood" to be shed in America.[3]

Ironically, however, at the very moment when victory in the Civil War should have proved conclusively the righteousness of the North, success blunted the Northern critique of the South. Having won the war, most Northerners no longer felt the need to demonstrate the superiority of their region. In the mainline churches especially, Christians interpreted the eradication of the evil of slavery and the preservation of the Union as clear, unmistakable proof of God's approval of Northern society. Even Beecher himself extended the right hand of fellowship to Southerners who would repent of their former sins. The North imagined that it had gained (again, to use a phrase of Robert Penn Warren) an inexhaustible Treasury of Virtue" in the conflict. Success had made Northerners complacent, and complacency in turn allowed them to be magnanimous to the South. They could well afford, it seemed, to be generous.[4]

Unlike their counterparts in the South, Northern churchmen devised an interpretation of the Civil War that did not dwell merely on the righteousness of their own section. Instead, they found in the conflict a message of universal and eternal importance. One of the most profound statements about the meaning of the war was presented by Horace Bushnell at Yale College in his 1865 commencement address entitled "Our Obligations to the Dead." Bushnell observed that Americans had once lacked a sense of identity as a nation, but they had discovered in the anguish of bloodshed and battle "a great consciousness and great public sentiments," which were the cornerstones of genuine nationhood. Continuing an argument that he had presented at the outset of the war, Bushnell noted that the United States might always have remained psychologically and

---

[3]Willie Lee Rose, *Rehearsal for Reconstruction: The Port Royal Experiment* (Indianapolis: The Bobbs-Merrill Co., Inc., 1964) 343; and Buck, *Road to Reunion*, 6-7, 72-73, 94-95, 234.

[4]Robert Penn Warren, *The Legacy of the Civil War: Meditations on the Centennial* (New York: Random House, 1961) 59.

intellectually divided. The blood that Union soldiers had shed, however, washed away the theoretical distinctions separating Americans, and the sacrifices of the battlefield had atoned for all the nation's past sins. Those soldiers were "the victims in that great sacrifice of blood" that had "cemented and sanctified" American unity and "consecrated our free institutions." The war represented "the grandest chapter" of all human history, for the ideals made incarnate in the Constitution of the United States, Bushnell claimed, were the same principles upon which the Kingdom of God was based.[5]

The United States seemed to stand triumphant as the guardian of civil and religious liberty, a beacon of freedom in a benighted world. Many churchmen in the North believed that the war had been a providential event that prepared their country to champion libertarian ideals in even greater crusades. Religious aspirations concerning America as a nation rose to a peak at the close of the Civil War, because despite the war's testing the assumption that God called the United States to a special mission, the triumph of the Union confirmed that this belief was valid. Northerners asserted that the Civil War had been an apocalyptic struggle that had resolved internal problems long vexing the American people. As a result of their wartime accomplishments, Northern spokesmen looked beyond the successful mission in the South and sought new fields in which to labor. No longer principally concerned with issues involving the Civil War, the Northern mainline churches in the last decades of the century carried their religious and political message into other areas: the organization of revivals to convert the American cities, the redemption of the underprivileged from oppressing social conditions, and the evangelistic outreach to the heathen overseas.[6]

The figure of Abraham Lincoln also became prominent in this period, when religious leaders in the North turned their attention away from issues that had attracted them during the war itself. During his life, Lincoln had profoundly articulated the moral dilemmas that his nation faced, and he had made the idea of the Union a virtually mystical cause. Through his death on Good Friday in 1865, moreover, Lincoln served as a symbolic propitiation

---

[5][Mary Bushnell Cheney], *Life and Letters of Horace Bushnell* (New York: Charles Scribner's Sons, 1903) 486-87; James H. Moorhead, *American Apocalypse: Yankee Protestants and the Civil War, 1860-1869* (New Haven: Yale University Press, 1978) 169-71; and William A. Clebsch, *From Sacred to Profane America: The Role of Religion in American History* (New York: Harper and Row, 1968) 193-96.

[6]Clebsch, *From Sacred to Profane America,* 188-99; and Moorhead, *American Apocalypse,* 219-29.

for the evil he had conquered. In the public eye he became a martyr, a saint, and—most significantly—an image of forgiveness. Like Christ forgiving his afflicters at the moment of his death, so Lincoln forgave the people who murdered him. Having suffered the griefs and agonies of a war in which he sent thousands of young Americans to die, he confirmed his good faith in that cause by laying down his own life with those men. Thus, he figuratively banished vindictiveness from the Northern mind and encouraged a more all-embracing understanding of the Civil War. Lincoln was a symbol of the conjunction of biblical concepts and American cultural ideals, and his death at the war's end appeared to confirm the eschatological significance that Northern churchmen had invested in the struggle against the South. Lincoln represented a perfect fulfillment of everything the North had hoped to gain; he had destroyed slavery, preserved the Union, and provided an image of sacrifice and rebirth.[7]

The North, in fact, received *too* much good fortune, and its wartime successes engendered unrealistic expectations about what Americans could accomplish. Northerners had been tempted into exaggerating their national achievements, and when they failed to attain the superhuman goals they set for themselves, many were left disillusioned. The national glories that churchmen foretold simply never materialized. Instead, the era of Reconstruction was marked by extreme disappointment and a sense of failure, and social and political turmoil were distressing facts of life. Within the Northern churches themselves, traditional religious beliefs were thought to be under attack by a variety of adversaries, the comparative study of religion undercut the uniqueness of Christianity, and liberal theologians seemed to be smoothing away the edges of orthodoxy and rejecting the idea of a changeless faith. Amid the materialism and secularism that characterized the Gilded Age, many ordinary Christians vainly sought reassurance that the faith they held was true.[8]

Jackson Lears's fine study of late nineteenth- and early twentieth-century American culture has illuminated the feelings of doubt that undermined the "official" liberal optimism of that time. A sense of human finitude survived in the North both despite and because of the war. Victory could never remove the presence of Civil War veterans, not only the formerly magnificent now aging heroes, but also the men who had been

---

[7]Edmund Wilson, *Patriotic Gore: Studies in the Literature of the American Civil War* (Boston: Northeastern University Press, 1984) 97-98, 130; and John F. Wilson, *Public Religion in American Culture* (Philadelphia: Temple University Press, 1979) 12-13.

[8]Paul A. Carter, *The Spiritual Crisis of the Gilded Age* (DeKalb: Northern Illinois University Press, 1971) 6, 10, 65-67; and Moorhead, *American Apocalypse,* 236-44.

physically and emotionally scarred by their experiences in battle. Nor could Americans ignore the apparent arbitrariness of existence itself, in which disease and infection still could claim the lives of the heretofore youthful and healthy. The optimism of the 1860s, then, had been transformed in twenty years to an ideal that seemed false and untenable. The world looked no better at the end of the century than it had at midcentury, while the social stability of the antebellum period seemed more desirable in comparison to the confusion and discord of the present day. Many in the North chose not to look forward, but began to seek in the past a balance to the excesses of the Gilded Age.[9]

The myth of the Lost Cause and the New South ethos that Southerners were fashioning at this time provided powerful symbols that helped recall Northerners from the moral void they thought they were facing. Just when Northern myths about the meaning of the war had permanently lost their credibility, Southern legends caught the imagination of Americans in every section of the country, and these legends proved to have an important impact on the development of American religious thought. Although much has been written about so-called "unreconstructed Southern rebels," most Southerners made haste to swear allegiance to the Union again. And even the postwar Southern myths flourished within the safe confines of a reunited nation. The Lost Cause gave the South the sense of honor it sought, and the North easily conceded that point to its former adversary. Southern writers appealing to Northern audiences to trust their depictions of religious fervor in the Confederate camp had found the believers they sought.[10]

The use of the figure of Cromwell and his Roundheads in Southern writings about the religious life of the Confederate armies took on a special significance at this time. In order to describe the quality of their military leadership, clerical interpreters of the Lost Cause insisted that Cromwell—the stern Puritan, a man of unconquerable strength in battle and unmatched piety—best described the typical Southern soldier. Through their willingness to use this metaphor, Southern clergymen virtually reversed the traditional paradigm of the Cavalier South and the Puritan North. Before the war, the so-called "Puritan Ethic" had by no means been out of place in the South, and although a positive view of the Puritans had fallen out of favor in the Confederacy between 1860 and 1865,

---

[9]T. J. Jackson Lears, *No Place of Grace: Antimodernism and the Transformation of American Culture* (New York: Pantheon Books, 1981) 4-5, 25-26.

[10]Kenneth M. Stampp, *The Imperiled Union: Essays on the Background of the Civil War* (New York: Oxford University Press, 1980) 266.

the results of the war made that image acceptable again among Southern church members. In their postwar treatises in defense of the Southern way of life, Southerners argued that, while the descendants of the Puritans of New England had abandoned their religious heritage and become licentious and unfaithful, descendants of the original settlers in the Southern states upheld theological orthodoxy in America. Southerners interpreted the American Civil War in light of the same moral principles over which the English Civil War had been fought. They declared, hoever, that *they* were the Puritans who stood for true piety against the forces of worldliness and irreligion that held sway over the North.[11]

J. William Jones, for instance, continually repeated in his writings that all the Southern armies, and the Army of Northern Virginia in particular, had been "Roundhead" armies. Indeed, Jones claimed that Lee's soldiers had been more religious than Cromwell's, for the Southern churches were unique in the way they nurtured the faith men brought with them into the camp. (American religion, after all, was entirely free of the corrupting taints that marked even the highest forms of religious belief in the Old World.) This theme was repeated on numerous occasions in articles that appeared in the *Southern Historical Society Papers*. One such piece recorded the address by a former Confederate officer to an assembly of Southern veterans. The officer praised the men for having belonged to such a pious army, from which one might "draw a picture of faith and trust and loyalty, such as the world has not seen since Cromwell's army." The presence of Christians throughout every rank of the Southern army, he said, had made it an unmatched moral and religious force.[12]

The symbol of the Puritan soldier enabled Southern Christians to reconcile themselves to the outcome of the war, reassert the moral superi-

---

[11]Charles Reagan Wilson, *Baptized in Blood: The Religion of the Lost Cause, 1865-1920* (Athens: University of Georgia Press, 1980) 44; Richard T. Hughes, "A Civic Theology for the South: The Case of Benjamin M. Palmer," *Journal of Church and State* 25 (1983): 450-51; C. Vann Woodward, "The Southern Ethic in a Puritan World," in *Myth and Southern History: The Old South*, ed. Patrick Gerster and Nicholas Cords (Chicago: Rand McNally College Publishing Company, 1974) 38-42; and Daniel R. Hundley, *Social Relations in Our Southern States*, ed. William J. Cooper, Jr. (Baton Rouge: Louisiana State University Press, 1979) 91-93. For an extended analysis of the Puritan ideal in American thought, see Jan C. Dawson, *The Unusable Past: America's Puritan Tradition, 1830 to 1930* (Chico CA: Scholars Press, 1984).

[12]J. William Jones, *Christ in the Camp; or, Religion in Lee's Army* (Richmond: B. F. Johnson & Co., 1887) 20; J. William Jones, "The Morale of the Confederate Army," in *Confederate Military History*, ed. Clement A. Evans (Atlanta: Confederate Publishing Co., 1899) 12:148-49; and John Lamb, "The Character and Services of the Confederate Soldier," *Southern Historical Society Papers* 40 (1915): 231, 237.

ority of the South, and link Southern society—at least in a figurative
fashion—back to the mainstream of American life. This image was also
effective in convincing Americans everywhere of the religious strength of
the defeated South. The positive reappraisal of the Puritan tradition and
nostalgic backward glances at the settling of America seemed to be the
perfect remedy for Americans who wished to blot out of their minds the
venality and infidelity that marked the Gilded Age. Some Northerners
even blamed the war, the moral crusade that should have sealed forever
the special relationship between God and America, for bringing more
prosperity than the North could responsibly handle. In this context, the
Puritan ethic of moderation and hard work appeared quite attractive, and
many saw in that legacy a set of ideals that could be applied to all cultures
and situations. The clerical apologists of the Lost Cause not only took advantage of this popular symbol, but they also gave it fuller shape in their
application of it to Confederate army life.[13]

While the myth of the Lost Cause maintained the legends of the past,
the creed of the New South added further ideological justification to claims
about Southern rectitude. In his "New South" speech, Henry Grady himself admitted that he was glad that the South had lost the war and spoke
glowingly of the reconciliation of Puritan and Cavalier after the Confederacy surrendered. This address, it turned out, created a flood of senti-
ment in its favor, for Grady was prepared to forget old hostilities and resume
the national task of making America great. He believed that the Puritan
and the Cavalier had, in fact, never really been so different, but represented two facets of the one American character. Abraham Lincoln actually was a hero for both sections of the country, for he was "the sum of
Puritan and Cavalier," containing the virtuous characteristics of each figure and the faults of neither. Grady looked as well to the former Confederate soldier, the "hero in gray with a heart of gold," as the perfect
embodiment of moral integrity and industriousness, an inspiration for
Americans everywhere. In the face of almost utter devastation, Southern
soldiers were not bitter, but all the more cheerful and hardworking. "Surely
God, who stripped [the soldier] of his prosperity," Grady mused, "inspired

---

[13]Wilson, *Baptized in Blood,* 84-88; Buck, *Road to Reunion,* 28; Rollin G. Osterweis,
The Myth of the Lost Cause, 1865-1900 (Hamden CT: Archon Books, 1973) 129; and C.
Vann Woodward, *Origins of the New South, 1877-1913,* vol. 9 of *A History of the South*
(Baton Rouge: Louisiana State University Press, 1951) 172.

him in his adversity. As ruin was never before so overwhelming, never was restoration swifter."[14]

Southerners like Grady and Jones insisted that their people had preserved a heritage that was valuable for all Americans, and they believed that the entire nation could benefit from attention to the enduring religious values for which the South stood. The bright future Northern church leaders had envisioned never really emerged, and many in the North felt disillusioned by the sorry state of the United States in the postwar period. Northern Protestants in particular feared that the Civil War had uprooted a whole generation of men and had forever torn the country away from the virtues that once had shaped small-town American life. Thus, despite the failure of the Southerners' dream of a separate national identity, they still staunchly maintained their cultural identity and used their experience in the war as an important symbol of the worth of a traditionalistic religious faith. At the same time Northern religion had become confused, divided, and unable to find a cogent interpretation of its success in the war, Southern religion used its own sense of inferiority after the defeat as a rallying point to buttress its self-esteem. Religious life in the South never appeared stronger than it did at the end of the nineteenth century.

Ideas about the special fortitude of Southern religiosity ceased to be an exclusive preoccupation of Southerners and became instead a part of the mythology of the entire nation. Both Northerners and Southerners were looking for a kind of pastoral dreamland to which they hoped the country could return; the conjuring of romantic images of life in the Southern camps was an important element in the satisfaction of that wish. Religion, which once had played a role in breaking the nation apart, now aided the reunification of the South with the North. The Christlike Abraham Lincoln metaphorically embraced and forgave the equally forgiving figure of Christlike Robert E. Lee, while the spectral Stonewall Jackson, the stern Puritan warrior, made peace with the Puritan exemplars of New England. North and South had seemingly attained a perfect spiritual affinity.

Religion in the South emerged as an important bulwark of Southern culture and was to have a telling influence on American society as a whole. The Southerners' insistence that their churches should remain aloof from the vagaries of political and social concerns proved—in the end—to be a more enduring ideal than the attempt of the Northern denominations to fashion a morally uniform society. During the war itself, religion in the

---

[14]Henry Grady, *The New South: Writings and Speeches of Henry Grady*, ed. Mills Lane (Savannah: Beehive Press, 1971) 4-7, 12; and Paul M. Gaston, *The New South Creed: A Study in Southern Mythmaking* (New York: Knopf, 1970) 90.

North had given its people the spiritual support they needed to win an otherwise arduous conflict, and its social ethic was a useful stimulus in prodding the Union to victory. Yet, Northern churchmen after 1865 were too well satisfied with what they had accomplished in the war. They not only lacked further incentive to prosecute an ideological battle against the South, but they also drastically overestimated their own ability to continue their earlier, hard-won successes. The otherworldly tenor of Southern Christianity, on the other hand, was best suited to a losing cause, for after the downfall of the Confederacy and amid the squalid materialism of the Gilded Age in the North, the churches remained relatively untouched as a powerful force for the revitalization of the South. Religion, therefore, helped foster both an attitude of stoic resignation throughout the South's doomed struggle for independence and a sense of regional superiority when the United States once again returned to peace.

BIBLIOGRAPHY

PRIMARY SOURCES

MANUSCRIPT COLLECTIONS

Capers, Ellison. Papers. Manuscript Department, Duke University Library, Durham NC.

————. Papers. Jessie Ball DuPont Library, University of the South, Sewanee TN.

Dabney, Robert Lewis. Papers. Historical Foundation of the Presbyterian and Reformed Churches, Montreat NC.

————. Papers. Southern Historical Collection, Library of the University of North Carolina at Chapel Hill.

————. Papers. Union Theological Seminary, Richmond VA.

Eddy, Richard. Papers. Andover-Harvard Theological Library, Harvard Divinity School, Cambridge MA.

Elliott, Stephen. Papers. Jessie Ball DuPont Library, University of the South, Sewanee TN.

Higginson, Thomas Wentworth. Papers. Houghton Library, Harvard University, Cambridge MA.

Hill, Daniel Harvey. Papers. Southern Historical Collection, Library of the University of North Carolina at Chapel Hill.

Hoge, Moses Drury. Papers. Henry E. Huntington Library, San Marino CA.

————. Papers. Virginia Historical Society, Richmond VA.

Hoge Family. Papers. Historical Foundation of the Presbyterian and Reformed Churches, Montreat NC.

Kennedy, Francis M. Papers. Southern Historical Collection, Library of the University of North Carolina at Chapel Hill.

Lacy, Beverly Tucker. Papers. Southern Historical Collection, Library of the University of North Carolina at Chapel Hill.

Lacy, Drury. Papers. Southern Historical Collection, Library of the University of North Carolina at Chapel Hill.

Otey, James H. Papers. Jessie Ball DuPont Library, University of the South, Sewanee TN.

Palmer, Benjamin Morgan. Papers. Historical Foundation of the Presbyterian and Reformed Churches, Montreat NC.

Pendleton, William Nelson. Papers. Southern Historical Collection, Library of the University of North Carolina at Chapel Hill.

Polk, Leonidas. Papers. Southern Historical Collection, Library of the University of North Carolina at Chapel Hill.

_____. Papers. Jessie Ball DuPont Library, University of the South, Sewanee TN.

Quintard, Charles Todd. Papers. Manuscript Department, Duke University Library, Durham NC.

_____. Papers. Jessie Ball DuPont Library, University of the South, Sewanee TN.

Russell, William. Papers. Manuscript Department, Duke University Library, Durham NC.

Street, James K. Papers. Southern Historical Collection, Library of the University of North Carolina at Chapel Hill.

United States Christian Commission. Records. National Archives, Washington DC.

ECCLESIASTICAL RECORDS

American Baptist Home Missionary Society. *Annual Report* 29-33 (1861-1865).

American Home Missionary Society. *Report,* 35-39 (1861-1865).

American Tract Society (New England Branch). *Annual Report* 3 (1862) and 5 (1864).

American Unitarian Association. *Annual Report* 36-40 (1861-1865).

Bible Society of Massachusetts. *Annual Report* 52-55 (1861-1864).

Cumberland Presbyterian Church. *Minutes of the General Assembly* 31-35 (1861-1865).

Massachusetts Baptist Convention. *Annual Report* 59-63 (1861-1865).

Massachusetts Bible Society. *Annual Report* 56 (1865).

Methodist Episcopal Church. *Journal of the General Conference,* 1864.

Presbyterian Church in the Confederate States of America. *Minutes of the General Assembly,* 1863-1864.

Presbyterian Church in the United States (South). *Minutes of the General Assembly,* 1865.

Presbyterian Church in the United States of America (New School). *Minutes of the General Assembly* 12-14 (1861-1862, 1865).

Presbyterian Church in the United States of America (Old School). *Minutes and Reports of the General Assembly* 16-17 (1861-1865).

Protestant Episcopal Church in the Confederate States of America. *Journals.* Centenary edition in facsimile. Edited by William A. Clebsch. Austin TX: Church Historical Society, 1962.

Protestant Episcopal Church in the United States of America. *Journal of the General Convention*, 1862.

Southern Baptist Convention. *Proceedings of the Ninth Biennial Sessions*, 1863.

Synod of North Carolina (Presbyterian). *Minutes*, 1861-1863.

Synod of South Carolina (Presbyterian). *Minutes*, 1861-1863.

Synod of Virginia (Presbyterian). *Minutes*, 1861-1865.

United States Christian Commission. *Annual Report* 1-4 (1862-1865).

JOURNALS

American Missionary 5-9 (1861-1865).

The Church Intelligencer 2-5 (1861-1865).

The Congregational Quarterly 3-7 (1861-1865).

The Danville Quarterly Review 1-4 (1861-1864).

Harper's Weekly 5-9 (1861-1865).

The Home Missionary 34-37 (1861-1865).

The Land We Love 1-6 (1866-1869).

Methodist Quarterly Review 43-47 (1861-1865).

The Monthly Journal of the American Unitarian Association 2-6 (1861-1865).

The Monthly Religious Magazine 26-33 (1861-1865).

The National Preacher, New Series, 4-6 (1861-1863).

The Religious Herald 34-38 (1861-1865).

Richmond Christian Advocate 20-21 (1862-1865).

Southern Churchman 28-30 (1862-1864).

Southern Presbyterian Review 14-16 (1861-1866).

Southern Historical Society Papers 1-52 (1876-1959).

Western Christian Advocate 30-31 (1863-1864).

BOOKS AND ARTICLES (THE NORTH)

Adams, John R. *Memorial and Letters of Rev. John R. Adams, D. D.* Cambridge MA: Privately printed, 1890.

Bartol, Cyrus A. *The Purchase by Blood: A Tribute to Brig.-Gen. Charles Russell Lowell, Jr.* Boston: John Wilson and Son, 1864.

——————— . *The Remission by Blood: A Tribute to Our Soldiers and the Sword, Delivered in the West Church.* Boston: Walker, Wise, and Company, 1862.

Berlin, Ira, ed. *The Black Military Experience. Freedom, A Documentary History of Emancipation, 1861-1867,* series 2. Cambridge: Cambridge University Press, 1982.

Billingsley, Amos S. *From the Flag to the Cross: or, Scenes and Incidents of Christianity in the War.* Philadelphia: New-World Publishing Company, 1872.

Boyd, Cyrus F. *The Civil War Diary of Cyrus F. Boyd: Fifteenth Iowa Infantry, 1861-1863.* Edited by Mildred Throne. Millwood NY: Kraus Reprint Co., 1977.

Brainerd, Cephas. *The Work of the Army Committee of the New York Young Men's Christian Association.* New York: John Medole, 1866.

Brainerd, Thomas. *Remarks of Rev. Dr. Brainerd at the Funeral of Lieut. John T. Greble, U. S. A.* Philadelphia: G. T. Stockdale, 1861.

Bristol, Frank Milton. *The Life of Chaplain McCabe, Bishop of the Methodist Episcopal Church.* New York: Fleming H. Revell, Co., 1908.

Brooks, Elbridge G. "Our Civil War." *Universalist Quarterly* 17 (1861): 251-77.

Brown, William Y. *The Army Chaplain: His Office, Duties, and Responsibilities, and the Means of Aiding Him.* Philadelphia: W. S. & A. Martien, 1863.

Bushnell, Horace. *Building Eras in Religion.* New York: Charles Scribner's Sons, 1881.

——————. *Reverses Needed: A Discourse Delivered on the Sunday after the Disaster of Bull Run.* Hartford: L. E. Hunt, 1861.

[Cheney, Mary Bushnell.] *Life and Letters of Horace Bushnell.* New York: Charles Scribner's Sons, 1903.

Christ in the Army: Selection of Sketches of the Work of the U.S. Christian Commission. Philadelphia: Ladies Christian Commission, 1865.

"Christianity in the Army." *The Christian Register* 47 (11 July 1868): 2.

Clark, Charles M. *The History of the Thirty-Ninth Regiment, Illinois Volunteer Veteran Infantry.* Chicago: Veteran Association of the Regiment, 1889.

Connolly, James A. *Three Years in the Army of the Cumberland: The Letters and Diary of Major James A. Connolly.* Edited by Paul M. Angle. Bloomington: Indiana University Press, 1959.

Corby, William. *Memoirs of Chaplain Life.* Notre Dame IN: "Scholastic" Press, 1894.

Curtis, Newton Martin. *From Bull Run to Chancellorsville: The Story of the Sixteenth New York Infantry Together with Personal Reminiscences.* New York: G. P. Putnam's Sons, 1906.

DeForest, John William. *A Volunteer's Adventures: A Union Captain's Record of the Civil War.* Edited by James H. Croushore. New Haven: Yale University Press, 1946.

Denison, Frederic. "A Chaplain's Experience in the Union Army." *Personal Narratives of Events in the War of the Rebellion, Being Papers Read before the Rhode Island Soldiers and Sailors Historical Society.* 4th series, 20. Providence: The Society, 1893.

Dodd, Ira S. *The Song of the Rappahannock: Sketches of the Civil War.* New York: Dodd, Mead, and Company, 1898.

Dunham, Albertus A. and Charles LaForest. *Through the South with a Union Soldier.* Edited by Arthur H. DeRosier, Jr. Johnson City TN: The East Tennessee State University, 1969.

[Dwight, Elizabeth A. W.] *Life and Letters of Wilder Dwight, Lieut.-Col. Second Mass. Inf. Vols.* Boston: Ticknor and Fields, 1868.

Eaton, John. *Grant, Lincoln, and the Freedmen: Reminiscences of the Civil War.* New York: Longmans, Green, and Co., 1907.

Eddy, Richard. *History of the Sixtieth New York State Volunteers.* Philadelphia: The author, 1864.

Edgar, Cornelius H. "Germs and Growth." In *Render unto Caesar: A Collection of Sermon Classics on All Phases of Religion in Wartime.* New York: Lewis Publishing Company, 1943.

Fisk, Wilbur. *Anti-Rebel: The Civil War Letters of Wilbur Fisk.* Croton-on-Hudson NY: Emil Rosenblatt, 1983.

Fuller, Richard Frederick. *Chaplain Fuller: Being a Life Sketch of a New England Clergyman and Army Chaplain.* Boston: Walker, Wise and Co., 1863.

Gage, Moses D. *From Vicksburg to Raleigh; or, A Complete History of the Twelfth Regiment Indiana Volunteer Infantry.* Chicago: Clarke & Co., 1865.

Gladden, Washington. *Recollections.* Boston: Houghton Mifflin Company, 1909.

Hale, Edward Everett. *The Desert and the Promised Land: A Sermon.* Boston: C. C. P. Moody, 1863.

————. *The Future Civilization of the South: A Sermon.* Boston: N.p., 1862.

Hammond, Jonathan Pinkney. *The Army Chaplain's Manual, Designed as a Help to Chaplains in the Discharge of Their Various Duties.* Philadelphia: J. B. Lippincott & Co., 1863.

Higginson, Thomas Wentworth. *Army Life in a Black Regiment.* New York: W. W. Norton & Company, 1984.

————. *Cheerful Yesterdays.* Boston: Houghton, Mifflin and Company, 1898.

————. *Letters and Journals of Thomas Wentworth Higginson, 1846-1906.* Edited by Mary Thacher Higginson. New York: Da Capo Press, 1969.

Hight, John J. *History of the Fifty-Eighth Regiment of Indiana Volunteer Infantry.* Compiled by Gilbert R. Stormont. Princeton IN: Press of the Clarion, 1895.

Holmes, John Haynes. *The Life and Letters of Robert Collyer, 1823-1912,* 2 vols. New York: Dodd, Mead and Company, 1917.

Howard, Oliver Otis. *Autobiography of Oliver Otis Howard, Major General United States Army,* 2 vols. Freeport NY: Books for Libraries Press, 1971.

_____. *Major-General Howard's Address at the Second Anniversary of the U.S. Christian Commission.* Philadelphia: Caxton Press, 1864.

Howard, Philip Eugene. *The Life Story of Henry Clay Trumbull: Missionary, Army Chaplain, Editor, and Author.* Philadelphia: The Sunday School Times, 1905.

Humphreys, Charles A. *Field, Camp, Hospital and Prison in the Civil War, 1863-1865.* Boston: George H. Ellis Co., 1918.

Kircher, Henry A. *A German in the Yankee Fatherland: The Civil War Letters of Henry A. Kircher.* Edited by Earl J. Hess. Kent OH: The Kent State University Press, 1983.

Locke, William Henry. *The Story of the Regiment.* New York: James Miller, 1872.

MacCauley, Clay. *Memories and Memorials: Gatherings from an Eventful Life.* Tokyo: The Fukuin Printing Co., Ltd., 1914.

Marks, James Junius. *The Peninsular Campaign in Virginia, or Incidents and Scenes on the Battle-Fields and in Richmond.* Philadelphia: J. B. Lippincott Company, 1864.

McAllister, Robert. *The Civil War Letters of General Robert McAllister.* Edited by James I. Robertson, Jr. New Brunswick NJ: Rutgers University Press, 1965.

McClellan, George B. *McClellan's Own Story: The War for the Union.* New York: Charles L. Webster and Company, 1887.

Mohr, James C., ed. *The Cormany Diaries: A Northern Family in the Civil War.* Pittsburgh: University of Pittsburgh Press, 1982.

Moss, Lemuel. *Annals of the United States Christian Commission.* Philadelphia: J. B. Lippincott & Co., 1868.

Patrick, Marsena Rudolf. *Inside Lincoln's Army: The Diary of Marsena Rudolf Patrick, Provost Marshal General, Army of the Potomac.* Edited by David S. Sparks. New York: Thomas Yoseloff, 1964.

Quint, Alonzo H. *The Potomac and the Rapidan: Army Notes.* Boston: Crosby and Nichols, 1864.

_____. *The Record of the Second Massachusetts Infantry, 1861-1865.* Boston: James P. Walker, 1867.

Rogers, James B. *War Pictures: Experiences and Observations of a Chaplain in the U.S. Army in the War of the Southern Rebellion.* Chicago: Church & Goodman, 1863.

Schurz, Carl. *The Reminiscences of Carl Shurz*, 3 vols. New York: The McClure Company, 1906-1908.

Small, Abner R. *The Road to Richmond: The Civil War Memoirs of Major Abner R. Small of the Sixteenth Maine Regiment.* Edited by Harold Adams Small. Berkeley: University of California Press, 1939.

Smith, Edward Parmelee. *Incidents of the United States Christian Commission.* Philadelphia: J. B. Lippincott & Co., 1869.

Stanton, Robert L. *The Church and the Rebellion: A Consideration of the Rebellion . . . and the Agency of the Church, North and South, in Relation Thereto.* Freeport NY: Books for Libraries Press, 1971.

Stevens, Emory M. "Story of the Chaplain." In *The Story of Our Regiment: A History of the 148th Pennsylvania Vols.*, edited by J. W. Muffly, 191-227. Des Moines IA: The Kenyon Printing & Mfg. Co., 1904.

Strong, George Templeton. *The Diary of George Templeton Strong.* Volume 3, *The Civil War, 1860-1865.* Edited by Allan Nevins and Milton Halsey Thomas. New York: The Macmillan Company, 1952.

Stuart, George H. *The Life of George H. Stuart.* Edited by Robert Ellis Thompson. Philadelphia: J. M. Stoddart & Co., 1890.

Tourgee, Albion W. *The Story of a Thousand, Being a History of the Service of the 105th Ohio Volunteer Infantry.* Buffalo: S. McGerald and Son, 1896.

Trumbull, Henry Clay. *The Captured Scout of the Army of the James: A Sketch of the Life of Sergeant Henry H. Manning of the Twenty-Fourth Mass. Regiment.* Boston: Nichols and Noyes, 1869.

_____. *Desirableness of Active Service: A Sermon Preached to the Tenth Connecticut Regiment.* Hartford: Case, Lockwood and Company, 1864.

_____. *Good News! A Sermon to the Veteran Volunteers of the 10th Connecticut Regiment.* Hartford: Case, Lockwood and Company, 1864.

_____. *A Good Record: A Sermon Preached . . . to the Tenth Connecticut Regiment.* Hartford: Case, Lockwood and Company, 1864.

_____. *War Memories of an Army Chaplain.* Philadelphia: Charles Scribner's Sons, 1898.

United States Christian Commission. *Address of the Christian Commission.* New York: Office of the Christian Commission, 1862

_____. *Christian Commission for the Army and Navy of the United States of America.* Philadelphia: Ringwalt & Brown, 1862.

United States War Department. *The War of the Rebellion: A Compilation of the Official Records of the Union and Confederate Armies*, 128 vols. Washington DC: Government Printing Office, 1880-1901.

Wadsworth, Charles. *War a Discipline: A Sermon Preached in Calvary Church, San Francisco.* San Francisco: H. H. Bancroft and Company, 1864.

Wormeley, Katherine Prescott. *The Other Side of War with the Army of the Potomac.* Boston: Ticknor and Company, 1889.

————. *The United States Sanitary Commission: A Sketch of Its Purposes and Its Works.* Boston: Little, Brown and Company, 1863.

BOOKS AND ARTICLES (THE SOUTH)

Anderson, G. W. "Religion in the Confederate Army." *Confederate Veteran* 6 (1898): 579.

Army and Navy Messenger for the Trans-Mississippi Department, 2 March 1865.

Atkinson, Joseph M. *God, the Giver of Victory and Peace: A Thanksgiving Sermon.* [Raleigh NC]: N.p., 1862.

B., Mrs. L. N. (of Macon GA). *The Christian Soldier the True Hero: Respectfully Dedicated to the Soldiers of the Confederate States.* Charleston: South Carolina Tract Society, [186—].

Bennett, William W. *A Narrative of the Great Revival Which Prevailed in the Southern Armies during the Late Civil War between the States of the Federal Union.* Philadelphia: Claxton, Remsen & Haffelfinger, 1877.

Caldwell, J. F. J. *The History of a Brigade of South Carolinians, Known First as "Gregg's," and Subsequently as "McGowan's Brigade."* Dayton OH: Morningside Bookshop, 1974.

The Camp and the Cross. Richmond: Soldiers' Tract Association, M. E. Church, South, [186—].

Casler, John D. *Four Years in the Stonewall Brigade,* 4th edition. Edited by James I. Robertson, Jr. Dayton OH: Morningside Bookshop, 1971.

Chamberlayne, John Hampden. *Ham Chamberlayne—Virginian: Letters and Papers of an Artillery Officer in the War for Southern Independence, 1861-1865.* Edited by C. G. Chamberlayne. Richmond: The Dietz Printing Co., Publishers, 1932.

Chesnut, Mary Boykin. *Mary Chesnut's Civil War.* Edited by C. Vann Woodward. New Haven: Yale University Press, 1981.

Christian. W. H. *The Importance of a Soldier Becoming a Christian.* Richmond: Soldiers' Tract Association, M. E. Church, South, [186—].

Cooke, John Esten. *Stonewall Jackson: A Military Biography.* New York: D. Appleton and Company, 1866.

————. *Stonewall Jackson and the Old Stonewall Brigade.* Edited by Richard B. Harwell. Charlottesville: University of Virginia Press, 1954.

————. *Wearing of the Gray; Being Personal Portraits, Scenes and Adventures of the War.* New York: E. B. Treat & Co., 1867.

Dabney, Robert Lewis. *The Christian Soldier: A Sermon Commemorative of the Death of Abram C. Carrington.* Richmond: Presbyterian Committee of Publication, 1863.

_____. *Life and Campaigns of Lieut.-Gen. Thomas J. Jackson.* New York: Blelock & Co., 1866.

_____. *A Memorial of Lieut. Colonel John T. Thornton, of the Third Virginia Cavalry, C. S. A.* Richmond: Presbyterian Committee of Publication, 1864.

_____. *True Courage: A Discourse Commemorative of Lieut. General Thomas J. Jackson.* Richmond: Presbyterian Committee of Publication, 1863.

DuBose, William Porcher. *Turning Points in My Life.* New York: Longmans, Green and Co., 1912.

Eggleston, George Cary. *A Rebel's Recollections.* Edited by David Donald. Bloomington: Indiana University Press, 1959.

Elliott, Stephen. *Ezra's Dilemna* [sic]: *A Sermon Preached in Christ Church, Savannah, on Friday, August 21st, 1863.* Savannah: George N. Nichols, 1863.

_____. "Funeral Sermon Preached by the Rt. Revd. Stephen Elliott." *Historical Magazine of the Protestant Episcopal Church* 7 (1938): 407-18.

_____. *How to Renew Our National Strength: A Sermon Preached in Christ Church, Savannah, on Friday, November 15th, 1861.* Savannah: John M. Cooper & Co., 1861.

_____. "*New Wine Not To Be Put into Old Bottles*": *A Sermon Preached in Christ Church, Savannah, on Friday, February 28th, 1862.* Savannah: John M. Cooper & Co., 1862.

_____. *Our Cause in Harmony with the Purposes of God in Christ Jesus: A Sermon Preached in Christ Church, Savannah, on Thursday, September 18th, 1862.* Savannah: John M. Cooper & Co., 1862.

Fitzgerald, Oscar P. *John B. McFerrin: A Biography.* Nashville: Publishing House of the M. E. Church, South, 1888.

Gordon, John Brown. *Reminiscences of the Civil War.* New York: Charles Scribner's Sons, 1903.

Gorgas, Josiah. *The Civil War Diary of General Josiah Gorgas.* Edited by Frank E. Vandiver. Huntsville: University of Alabama Press, 1947.

Grady, Henry. *The New South: Writings and Speeches of Henry Grady.* Edited by Mills Lane. Savannah: Beehive Press, 1971.

Holmes, Emma. *The Diary of Miss Emma Holmes, 1861-1866.* Edited by John F. Marszalek. Baton Rouge: Louisiana State University Press, 1979.

Hundley, Daniel R. *Prison Echoes of the Great Rebellion.* New York: S. W. Green, 1874.

_____. *Social Relations in Our Southern States.* Edited by William J. Cooper, Jr. Baton Rouge: Louisiana State University Press, 1979.

Inzer, John Washington. *The Diary of a Confederate Soldier: John Washington Inzer, 1834-1928.* Edited by Mattie Lou Teague Crow. Huntsville AL: The Strode Publishers, Inc., 1977.

Jackson, Mary Anna. *Memoirs of Stonewall Jackson by His Widow*. Louisville: The Prentice Press, 1895.

Johnson, Thomas Cary. *The Life and Letters of Robert Lewis Dabney*. Richmond: Presbyterian Committee of Publication, 1903.

————. *The Life and Letters of Benjamin Morgan Palmer*. Richmond: Presbyterian Committee of Publication, 1906.

Jones, J. William. *Army of Northern Virginia Memorial Volume*. Richmond: J. W. Randolph & English, 1880.

————. *Christ in the Camp; or, Religion in Lee's Army*. Richmond: B. F. Johnson & Co., 1887.

————. *Life and Letters of Robert Edward Lee, Soldier and Man*. New York: The Neale Publishing Company, 1906.

————. "The Morale of the Confederate Army." In *Confederate Military History*, edited by Clement A. Evans, 12:117-93. Atlanta: Confederate Publishing Company, 1899.

————. *Personal Reminiscences, Anecdotes, and Letters of Gen. Robert E. Lee*. New York: D. Appleton, 1875.

Jones, John B. *A Rebel War Clerk's Diary*. Edited by Earl Schenke Miers. New York: Sagamore Press, Inc., 1958.

Jones, Walter Burgwyn, ed. *Confederate War Poems*. Nashville: Bill Coats, Ltd., 1984.

McCarthy, Carlton. *Detailed Minutiae of Soldier Life in the Army of Northern Virginia, 1861-1865*. Richmond: B. F. Johnson Publishing Co., 1899.

McKim, Randolph Harrison. *In Memoriam: Good Men a Nation's Strength*. Baltimore: John Murphy & Co., 1870.

————. *The Motives and Aims of the Soldiers of the South in the Civil War*. Nashville: United Confederate Veterans, 1904.

————. *A Soldier's Recollections: Leaves from the Diary of a Young Confederate*. New York: Longmans, Green and Co., 1910.

————. *The Soul of Lee*. New York: Longmans, Green and Co., 1918.

Myers, Robert Manson, ed. *The Children of Pride: A True Story of Georgia and the Civil War*. New Haven: Yale University Press, 1972.

Nichols, G. W. *A Soldier's Story of His Regiment (61st Georgia)*. Kennesaw GA: Continental Book Company, 1961.

Nisbet, James Cooper. *4 Years on the Firing Line*. Edited by Bell Irvin Wiley. Jackson TN: McCowat-Mercer Press, Inc., 1963.

Nugent, William Lewis. *My Dear Nellie: The Civil War Letters of William L. Nugent to Eleanor Smith Nugent*. Edited by William M. Cash and Lucy Somerville Howorth. Jackson: University Press of Mississippi, 1977.

Owen, William Miller. *In Camp and Battle with the Washington Artillery of New Orleans.* Boston: Ticknor and Company, 1885.

Palmer, Benjamin Morgan. *Address Delivered at the Funeral of General Maxcy Gregg.* Columbia SC: Southern Guardian Steam-Power Press, 1863.

_____. *A Discourse before the General Assembly of South Carolina, on December 10, 1863.* Columbia SC: C. P. Pelham, 1864.

_____. *The Life and Letters of James Henley Thornwell, D. D., LL. D.* Richmond: Whittet & Shepperson, 1875.

_____. *The Oath of Allegiance to the United States, Discussed in Its Moral and Political Bearings.* Richmond: MacFarlanne & Ferguson, 1863.

_____. *Rights of the South Defended in the Pulpits.* Mobile: J. Y. Thompson, 1860.

Paris, John D. *A Sermon: Preached before Brig.-Gen. Hoke's Brigade, at Kinston, N.C., on the 28th of February, 1864.* Greensborough NC: A. W. Ingold & Co., 1864.

Patterson, Edmund DeWitt. *Yankee Rebel: The Civil War Journal of Edmund DeWitt Patterson.* Edited by John G. Barrett. Chapel Hill: The University of North Carolina Press, 1966.

Paxton, John Gallatin, ed. *The Civil War Letters of General Frank "Bull" Paxton, C. S. A.* Hillsboro TX: Hill Jr. College Press, 1978.

Pender, William Dorsey. *The General to His Lady: The Civil War Letters of William Dorsey Pender to Fanny Pender.* Edited by William W. Hassler. Chapel Hill: The University of North Carolina Press, 1965.

Polk, William M. *Leonidas Polk: Bishop and General,* 2 vols. New edition. New York: Longmans, Green and Co., 1915.

Pollard, Edward A. *The Lost Cause.* New York: E. B. Treat & Co., 1866.

Quintard, Charles Todd. *Doctor Quintard, Chaplain C. S. A. and Second Bishop of Tennessee; Being His Story of the War (1861-1865).* Edited by Arthur Howard Noll. Sewanee TN: The University Press, 1905.

Ruffin, Edmund. *The Diary of Edmund Ruffin,* 2 vols. Edited by William Kauffman Scarborough. Baton Rouge: Louisiana State University Press, 1972-1976.

Ryan, Abram Joseph. *Poems: Patriotic, Religious, Miscellaneous.* Baltimore: John B. Piet, 1880.

Stiles, Robert. *Four Years under Marse Robert.* New York: The Neale Publishing Co., 1903.

Taylor, Richard. *Destruction and Reconstruction: Personal Experiences of the Late Civil War.* Edited by Richard B. Harwell. New York: Longmans, Green and Co., 1955.

Thornwell, James Henley. *The Collected Writings of James Henley Thornwell, D. D., LL. D.,* 4 vols. Edited by John B. Adger and John L. Girardeau. Richmond: Presbyterian Committee of Publication, 1871-1873.

Watkins, Sam R. *"Co. Aytch,"* Maury Grays, First Tennessee Regiment; or, A Side Show of the Big Show. Edited by Bell Irvin Wiley. Jackson TN: McCowat-Mercer Press, 1952.

Wilmer, Richard Hooker. *Future Good—The Explanation of Present Reverses: A Sermon.* Charlotte NC: Protestant Episcopal Church Publishing Association, 1864.

————. *The Recent Past from a Southern Standpoint: Reminiscences of a Grandfather.* New York: T. Whittaker, 1887.

Wilson, LeGrand James. *The Confederate Soldier.* Edited by James W. Silver. Memphis: Memphis State University Press, 1973.

Worsham, John H. *One of Jackson's Foot Cavalry.* Edited by James I. Robertson, Jr. Jackson TN: McCowat-Mercer Press, Inc., 1964.

SECONDARY MATERIALS

Aaron, Daniel. *The Unwritten War: American Writers and the Civil War.* New York: Oxford University Press, 1975.

Ahlstrom, Sydney E. *A Religious History of the American People.* New Haven: Yale University Press, 1972.

Albrecht, Robert. "The Theological Response of the Transcendentalists to the Civil War." *New England Quarterly* 38 (1965): 21-34.

Alexander, Gross. *A History of the Methodist Church, South.* . . . Vol. 11 of *American Church History Series.* New York: The Christian Literature Co., 1894.

Anderson, Olive. "The Growth of Christian Militarism in Mid-Victorian England." *English Historical Review* 86 (1971): 46-72.

Atchison, Ray M. *"The Land We Love:* A Southern Post-Bellum Magazine of Agriculture, Literature, and Military History." *North Carolina Historical Review* 37 (1960): 506-16.

Bacon, Leonard. *A History of American Christianity.* Vol. 13 of *American Church History Series.* New York: The Christian Literature Co., 1898.

Barnes, Howard A. "The Idea That Caused a War: Horace Bushnell versus Thomas Jefferson." *Journal of Church and State* 16 (1974): 73-83.

Barton, Michael. *Goodmen: The Character of Civil War Soldiers.* University Park: Pennsylvania State University Press, 1981.

Bean, W. G. *The Liberty Hall Volunteers: Stonewall's College Boys.* Charlottesville: The University Press of Virginia, 1964.

Beringer, Richard E., et al., *Why the South Lost the Civil War.* Athens: The University of Georgia Press, 1986.

Blied, Benjamin J. *Catholics and the Civil War.* Milwaukee: N.p., 1945.

Blight, David W. "Frederick Douglass and the American Apocalypse." *Civil War History* 31 (1985): 309-28.

Boles, John B. *The Great Revival, 1787-1805: The Origins of the Southern Evangelical Mind.* Lexington: The University Press of Kentucky, 1972.

Bozeman, Theodore Dwight. "Science, Nature and Society: A New Approach to James Henley Thornwell." *Journal of Presbyterian History* 50 (1972): 307-25.

Bratton, Mary Jo. "John Esten Cooke and His 'Confederate Lies.' " *The Southern Literary Journal* 13 (1981): 72-91.

Brauer, Jerald C. "Regionalism and Religion in America." *Church History* 54 (1985): 366-78.

Bruce, Dickson D., Jr. *And They All Sang Hallelujah: Plain-Folk Camp-Meeting Religion, 1800-1845.* Knoxville: The University of Tennessee Press, 1974.

Buck, Paul H. *The Road to Reunion, 1865-1900.* Boston: Little, Brown and Company, 1947.

Cain, Marvin R. "A 'Face of Battle' Needed: An Assessment of Motives and Men in Civil War Historiography." *Civil War History* 28 (1982): 5-27.

Carpenter, John A. *Sword and Oliver Branch: Olive Otis Howard.* Pittsburgh: University of Pittsburgh Press, 1964.

Carter, Dan T. *When the War Was Over: The Failure of Self-Reconstruction in the South, 1865-1867.* Baton Rouge: Louisiana State University Press, 1985.

Carter, Paul A. *The Spiritual Crisis of the Gilded Age.* DeKalb: Northern Illinois University Press, 1971.

Childress, James F. *Moral Responsibility in Conflicts: Essays on Nonviolence, War, and Conscience.* Baton Rouge: Louisiana State University Press, 1982.

Clebsch, William A. "Baptism of Blood: A Study of Christian Contributions to the Interpretation of the Civil War in American History." Th.D. diss., Union Theological Seminary (New York) 1957.

_____. *Christian Interpretations of the Civil War.* Philadelphia: Fortress Press, 1969.

_____. *From Sacred to Profane America: The Role of Religion in American History.* New York: Harper and Row, 1968.

Colbenson, Pamela Elwyn Thomas. "Millennial Thought among Southern Evangelicals, 1830-1885." Ph. D. diss., Georgia State University, 1980.

Connelly, Thomas L. *The Marble Man: Robert E. Lee and His Image in American Society.* Baton Rouge: Louisiana State University Press, 1977.

Connelly, Thomas L. and Bellows, Barbara L. *God and General Longstreet: The Lost Cause and the Southern Mind.* Baton Rouge: Louisiana State University Press, 1982.

Dabbs, James McBride. *Haunted By God.* Richmond: John Knox Press, 1972.

Daniel, W. Harrison. "An Aspect of Church and State Relations in the Confederacy: Southern Protestantism and the Office of Army Chaplain." *North Carolina Historical Review* 36 (1959): 47-71.

————. "The Christian Association: A Religious Society in the Army of Northern Virginia." *Virginia Magazine of History and Biography* 69 (1961): 93-100.

————. "The Effects of the Civil War on Southern Protestantism." *Maryland Historical Magazine* 69 (1974): 44-63.

————. "Protestantism and Patriotism in the Confederacy." *Mississippi Quarterly* 24 (1971): 117-34.

————. "The Southern Baptists in the Confederacy." *Civil War History* 6 (1960): 389-401.

————. "Southern Protestantism and Army Missions in the Confederacy." *Mississippi Quarterly* 17 (1964): 179-91.

Davis, William C., ed. *The Image of War, 1861-1865.* Vol. 2, *The Guns of '62.* Garden City NY: Doubleday & Company, Inc., 1982.

Dawson, Jane C. *The Unusable Past: America's Puritan Tradition, 1830 to 1930.* Chico CA: Scholars Press, 1984.

Degler, Carl N. *Place over Time: The Continuity of Southern Distinctiveness.* Baton Rouge: Louisiana State University Press, 1977.

Denton, Charles Richard. "American Unitarians, 1830-1865: A Study of Religious Opinion on War, Slavery, and the Union." Ph. D. diss., Michigan State University, 1969.

Donald, David Herbert, ed. *Why the North Won the Civil War.* New York: Collier Books, 1973.

Ekman, Richard Howard. "Northern Religion and the Civil War." Ph. D. diss., Harvard University, 1972.

Eliot, Samuel A., ed. *Heralds of a Liberal Faith.* Vol. 3 , *The Preachers.* Boston: American Unitarian Association, 1910.

Farish, Hunter Dickinson. *The Circuit-Rider Dismounts. A Social History of Southern Methodism, 1865-1900.* New York: Da Capo Press, 1969.

Farmer, James Oscar, Jr. "The Metaphysical Confederacy; James Henley Thornwell and the Synthesis of Southern Values." Ph. D. diss., University of South Carolina, 1982.

Faulkner, William. *Absalom, Absalom!* New York: Vintage Books, 1972.

————. *The Unvanquished.* New York: Vintage Books, 1966.

Frassanito, William A. *Grant and Lee: The Virginia Campaigns, 1864-1865.* New York: Charles Scribner's Sons, 1983.

Fredrickson, George M. *The Inner Civil War: Northern Intellectuals and the Crisis of the Union.* New York: Harper & Row, 1968.

Gaston, Paul M. *The New South Creed: A Study in Southern Myth-Making.* New York: Knopf, 1970.

Genovese, Eugene D. *Roll, Jordan, Roll: The World the Slaves Made.* New York: Vintage Books, 1976.

Germain, Aidan Henry. *Catholic Military and Naval Chaplains, 1776-1917.* Washington DC: N. p., 1929.

Glatthaar, Joseph T. *The March to the Sea and Beyond: Sherman's Troops in the Savannah and Carolinas Campaign.* New York: New York University Press, 1985.

Goen, C. C. *Broken Churches, Broken Nation: Denominational Schisms and the Coming of the Civil War.* Macon GA: Mercer University Press, 1985.

Gravely, William. *Gilbert Haven, Methodist Abolitionist: A Study in Race, Religion, and Reform, 1850-1900.* Nashville: Abingdon Press, 1973.

Hattaway, Herman. *General Stephen D. Lee.* Jackson: University Press of Mississippi, 1976.

Hattaway, Herman and Jones, Archer. *How the North Won: A Military History of the Civil War.* Urbana: University of Illinois Press, 1983.

Henry, Joseph O. "The United States Christian Commission in the Civil War." *Civil War History* 6 (1960): 374-88.

Hieronymous, Frank L. "For Now and Forever: The Chaplains of the Confederate States Army." Ph. D. diss., University of California at Los Angeles, 1964.

Hill, Samuel S., Jr. *The South and the North in American Religion.* Athens: The University of Georgia Press, 1980.

Hill, Samuel S., Jr., ed. *Religion in the Southern States: A Historical Survey.* Macon GA: Mercer University Press, 1983.

Hobson, Fred. *Tell about the South: The Southern Rage to Explain.* Baton Rouge: Louisiana State University Press, 1983.

Holifield, E. Brooks. *The Gentlemen Theologians: American Theology in Southern Culture, 1795-1860.* Durham NC: Duke University Press, 1978.

Honeywell, Roy J. *Chaplains of the United States Army.* Washington DC: Office of the Chief of Chaplains, Department of the Army, 1958.

Hood, Fred J. *Reformed America: The Middle and Southern States, 1783-1837.* University: The University of Alabama Press, 1980.

Hughes, Richard T. "A Civic Theology for the South: The Case of Benjamin M. Palmer." *Journal of Church and State* 25 (1983): 447-67.

Johnson, Lorenzo D. *Chaplains of the General Government, With Objections to Their Employment Considered.* New York: Sheldon, Blakeman & Co., 1856.

Korn, Bertram Wallace. *American Jewry and the Civil War.* Philadelphia: Jewish Publications Society of America, 1951.

Kuykendall, John W. *Southern Enterprize: The Work of National Evangelical Societies in the Antebellum South.* Westport CT: Greenwood Press, 1982.

Lamers, William M. *The Edge of Glory: A Biography of General William S. Rose-crans, U. S. A.* New York: Harcourt, Brace & World, Inc., 1961.

Lears, T. J. Jackson. *No Place of Grace: Antimodernism and the Transformation of American Culture, 1880-1920.* New York: Pantheon Books, 1981.

Litwack, Leon F. *Been in the Storm So Long: The Aftermath of Slavery.* New York: Alfred A. Knopf, 1979.

Lively, Robert A. *Fiction Fights the Civil War: An Unfinished Chapter in the Literary History of the American People.* Chapel Hill: The University of North Carolina Press, 1957.

Loveland, Anne C. *Southern Evangelicals and the Social Order, 1880-1860.* Baton Rouge: Louisiana State University Press, 1980.

Luker, Ralph E. *A Southern Tradition in Theology and Social Criticism, 1830-1930: The Religious Liberalism and Social Conservatism of James Warley Miles, William Porcher DuBose and Edgar Gardner Murphy.* New York: The Edwin Mellen Press, 1984.

Maddex, Jack P. "From Theocracy to Spirituality: The Southern Presbyterian Reversal on Church and State." *Journal of Presbyterian History* 54 (1976): 438-57.

————. "Proslavery Millennialism: Social Eschatology in Antebellum Calvinism." *American Quarterly* 31 (1979): 46-62.

[Marsh, Catherine.] *Memorials of Captain Hedley Vicars, Ninety-Seventh Regiment.* New York: Protestant Episcopal Society for the Promotion of Evangelical Knowledge, 1857.

Marshman, John Clark. *Memoirs of Major-General Sir Henry Havelock, K. C. B.* 2nd edition. London: Longman, Green, Longman, and Roberts, 1861.

Mathews, Donald G. *Religion in the Old South.* Chicago: University of Chicago Press, 1977.

————. "The Second Great Awakening as an Organizing Process." *American Quarterly* 21 (1969): 23-43.

Maxwell, William Quentin. *Lincoln's Fifth Wheel: The Political History of the United States Sanitary Commission.* New York: Longmans, Green, 1956.

McCardell, John. *The Idea of a Southern Nation: Southern Nationalists and Southern Nationalism, 1830-1860.* New York: W. W. Norton & Company, 1979.

McCash, William B. *Thomas R. R. Cobb (1823-1862): The Making of a Southern Nationalist.* Macon GA: Mercer University Press, 1983.

McDonough, James Lee. *Chattanooga—A Death Grip on the Confederacy.* Knoxville: The University of Tennessee Press, 1984.

McFeely, William S. *Yankee Stepfather: General O. O. Howard and the Freedmen.* New Haven: Yale University Press, 1968.

McPherson, James M. *Ordeal by Fire: The Civil War and Reconstruction.* New York: Alfred A. Knopf, 1982.

Moorhead, James H. *American Apocalypse: Yankee Protestants and the Civil War, 1860-1869.* New Haven: Yale University Press, 1978.

Nolan, Alan T. *The Iron Brigade: A Military History.* Madison: The State Historical Society of Wisconsin, 1975.

Norton, Herman Albert. "The Organization and Function of the Confederate Military Chaplaincy, 1861-1865." Ph. D. diss., Vanderbilt University, 1956.

_____. *Struggling for Recognition: The United States Army Chaplaincy, 1791-1865.* History of the United States Army Chaplaincy, vol. 2. Washington DC: Office of the Chief of Chaplains, Department of the Army, 1977.

Oakes, James. *The Ruling Race: A History of American Slaveholders.* New York: Alfred A. Knopf, 1982.

Osterweis, Rollin G. *The Myth of the Lost Cause, 1865-1900.* Hamden CT: Archon Books, 1973.

Parish, Peter J. "The Instruments of Providence: Slavery, Civil War and the American Churches." In *The Church and War: Papers Read at the Twenty-First Summer Meeting and the Twenty-Second Winter Meeting of the Ecclesiastical History Society,* edited by W. J. Sheils, 291-320. Oxford: Basil Blackwell, 1983.

Parks, Joseph Howard. *General Edmund Kirby Smith. C. S. A.* Baton Rouge: Louisiana State University Press, 1954.

_____. *General Leonidas Polk, C. S. A.: The Fighting Bishop.* Baton Rouge: Louisiana State University Press, 1962.

Pressly, Thomas J. *Americans Interpret Their Civil War.* New York: The Free Press Books, 1962.

Prim, Gorrell Clinton, Jr. "Born Again in the Trenches: Revivalism in the Confederate Army." Ph. D. diss., Florida State University, 1982.

Quimby, Rollin W. "The Chaplains' Predicament." *Civil War History* 8 (1962): 25-37.

_____. "Congress and the Civil War Chaplaincy." *Civil War History* 10 (1964): 246-59.

_____. "Recurrent Themes and Purposes in the Sermons of Union Army Chaplains." *Speech Monographs* 31 (1964): 425-36.

Randall, James G. and Donald, David Herbert. *The Civil War and Reconstruction.* 2nd edition, revised. Lexington MA: D. C. Heath and Company, 1969.

Reynolds, Robert Lester. "Benevolence on the Home Front in Massachusetts during the Civil War." Ph. D. diss., Boston University, 1970.

Richardson, Joe M. *Christian Reconstruction: The American Missionary Association and Southern Blacks, 1861-1890.* Athens: University of Georgia Press, 1986.

Robertson, James I., Jr. "Chaplain William E. Wiatt: Soldier of the Cloth." In *Rank and File: Civil War Essays in Honor of Bell Irvin Wiley,* edited by James I. Robertson, Jr., and Richard M. McMurry, 113-36. San Rafael CA: Presidio Press, 1976.

_____. *Tenting Tonight: The Soldier's Life.* Alexandria VA: Time-Life Books, 1984.

Romero, Sidney J. *Religion in the Rebel Ranks.* Lanham MD: University Press of America, 1983.

Rose, Willie Lee. *Rehearsal for Reconstruction: The Port Royal Experiment.* Indianapolis: The Bobbs-Merrill Company, Inc., 1964.

Rowe, Anne. *The Enchanted Country: Northern Writers in the South, 1865-1910.* Baton Rouge: Louisiana State University Press, 1978.

Scott, Donald M. *From Office to Profession: The New England Ministry, 1750-1850.* Philadelphia: University of Pennsylvania Press, 1978.

Shattuck, Gardiner H., Jr. "A Shield and Hiding Place: The Religious Life of the Civil War Armies." Ph. D. diss., Harvard University, 1985.

Silver, James W. *Confederate Morale and Church Propaganda.* New York: W. W. Norton & Company, 1967.

Sizer, Sandra. "Politics and Apolitical Religion: The Great Urban Revivals of the Late Nineteenth Century." *Church History* 48 (1979): 81-98.

Smith, H. Shelton. *In His Image, But . . . : Racism in Southern Religion, 1780-1910.* Durham NC: Duke University Press, 1972.

Smith, Timothy L. *Revivalism and Social Reform: American Protestantism on the Eve of the Civil War.* Baltimore: Johns Hopkins University Press, 1980.

Spain, Rufus B. *At Ease in Zion: A Social History of Southern Baptists, 1865-1900.* Nashville: Vanderbilt University Press, 1967.

Stampp, Kenneth M. *The Imperiled Union: Essays on the Background of the Civil War.* New York: Oxford University Press, 1980.

Stange, Douglas C. "United for Sovereignty and Freedom: Unitarians and the Civil War." *Proceedings of the Unitarian Universalist Historical Society* 19 (1980-1981): 16-38.

Stokes, Anson Phelps. *Church and State in the United States,* 3 vols. New York: Harper & Brothers, 1950.

Stroupe, Henry Smith. *The Religious Press in the South Atlantic States, 1802-1865.* Durham NC: Duke University Press, 1956.

Sweet, Leonard I. " 'A Nation Born Again': The Union Prayer Meeting Revival and Cultural Revitalization." In *In the Great Tradition: Themes Honoring the Writings of Winthrop S. Hudson,* edited by Joseph D. Ban, 193-221. Valley Forge PA: Judson Press, 1982.

Sweet, William Warren. *The Methodist Episcopal Church and the Civil War.* Cincinnati: Methodist Book Concern Press, 1912.

_____. *The Story of Religions in America.* New York: Harper & Brothers, 1930.

Tate, Allen. "Remarks on the Southern Religion." In *I'll Take My Stand: The South and the Agrarian Tradition,* 155-75. New York: Harper Torchbooks, 1962.

Taylor, William. *Cavalier and Yankee: The Old South and American National Character.* Cambridge MA: Harvard University Press, 1979.

Thomas, Emory M. *The Confederate Nation, 1861-1865.* New York: Harper & Row Publishers, 1979.

Thompson, Ernest Trice. *The Spirituality of the Church: A Distinctive Doctrine of the Presbyterian Church in the United States.* Richmond: John Knox Press, 1961.

Tuveson, Ernest Lee. *Redeemer Nation: The Idea of America's Millennial Role.* Chicago: The University of Chicago Press, 1968.

Vander Velde, Lewis G. *The Presbyterian Churches and the Federal Union, 1861-1869.* Cambridge MA: Harvard University Press, 1932.

Warner, Ezra J. *Generals in Blue: Lives of the Union Commanders.* Baton Rouge: Louisiana State University Press, 1964.

_____. *Generals in Gray: Lives of the Confederate Commanders.* Baton Rouge: Louisiana State University Press, 1959.

Warren, Robert Penn. *The Legacy of the Civil War: Meditations on the Centennial.* New York: Random House, 1961.

Wight, Willard E. "Churches in the Confederacy." Ph. D. diss., Emory University, 1958.

Wiley, Bell Irvin. " 'Holy Joes' of the Sixties: A Study of Civil War Chaplains." *Huntington Library Quarterly* 16 (1953): 287-304.

_____. *The Life of Billy Yank: The Common Soldier of the Union.* Indianapolis: The Bobbs-Merrill Company, 1952.

_____. *The Life of Johnny Reb: The Common Soldier of the Confederacy.* Indianapolis: The Bobbs-Merrill Company, 1943.

Williams, George H. "The Chaplaincy in the Armed Forces of the United States of America in Historical and Ecclesiastical Perspective." In *Military Chaplains: From a Religious Military to a Military Religion,* edited by Harvey Cox, 11-39. New York: American Report Press, 1971.

Wilson, Charles Reagan. *Baptized in Blood: The Religion of the Lost Cause, 1865-1920.* Athens: University of Georgia Press, 1980.

Wilson, Charles Reagan, ed. *Religion in the South.* Jackson: University Press of Mississippi, 1985.

Wilson, Edmund. *Patriotic Gore: Studies in the Literature of the Civil War.* Boston: Northeastern University Press, 1984.

Wilson, John F. *Public Religion in American Culture.* Philadelphia: Temple University Press, 1979.

Woodward, C. Vann. *The Burden of Southern History.* Baton Rouge: Louisiana State University Press, 1960.

_____. *Origins of the New South, 1877-1913.* Vol. 9 of *A History of the South.* Baton Rouge: Louisiana State University Press, 1951.

————. "The Southern Ethic in a Puritan World." In *Myth and Southern History: The Old South,* edited by Patrick Gerster and Nicholas Cords, 31-56. Chicago: Rand McNally College Publishing Company, 1974.

Wyatt-Brown, Bertram. *Southern Honor: Ethics and Behavior in the Old South.* New York: Oxford University Press, 1982.

————. *Yankee Saints and Southern Sinners.* Baton Rouge: Louisiana State University Press, 1985.

INDEX